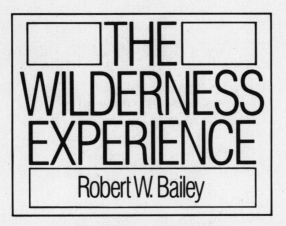

THE WILDERNESS EXPERIENCE

Robert W. Bailey

BROADMAN PRESS
Nashville, Tennessee

© Copyright 1989 • Broadman Press

All rights reserved

4250-78

ISBN: 0-8054-5078-5

Dewey Decimal Classification: 248.4

Subject Heading: CHRISTIAN LIFE

Scripture quotations are from the Revised Standard Version
of the Bible, copyrighted 1946, 1952, © 1971, 1973.

Library of Congress Catalog Card Number: 88-35271

Printed in the United States of America

Library of Congress Cataloging-in-Publication Data
Bailey, Robert W. (Robert Wilson), 1943-
The wilderness experience.

Bibliography: p.
1. Christian life.   2. Consolation.
I. Title.
BV4501.2.B29   1989   248.4'861   88-35271
ISBN 0-8054-5078-5

This book is dedicated to my family

Mary Frances, my wife
Kevin, my son
Courtney, my daughter
who have willingly journeyed into the wilderness with me
who have faithfully and consistently loved me and
who have encouraged and strengthened me
in my wilderness experiences

Contents

Introduction

A tourist visiting an apple orchard noticed some trees so weighted down with fruit they had to be propped up. He asked of the orchard owner: "What is the secret? How do you grow them so successfully?"

The grower responded, "I can't explain why, but I can tell you what happened."[1]

He pointed to the base of one of the largest apple trees and indicated an ugly scar that had partially healed during the past years. The visitor acknowledged the damage and questioned how it had happened. The owner explained, "In the beginning, too much of the tree was going to wood and not into fruit. We found that if we scarred the tree, we got less wood and more fruit. And we're in the fruit business."[2]

We are a people who avoid linking pain to growth.

We veer away from the reality of the relationship between struggle and productivity.

We hesitate to acknowledge that difficulties and stress have the potential of opening new doors to creativity.

Indeed, we are people who exist in a culture that promotes the "light" side of life and challenges its citizens to seek instant relief and cure of any of life's dark moments.

Yet, God is a God of contrasts. In Genesis we read that God separated darkness and light—yet He did not eliminate darkness. The world was without form, so God brought order

9

into chaos—yet He did not abolish all cases of chaos. We literally spend our lives seeking light, order, and purpose. But along the way there is darkness, chaos and crisis. Indeed, there is wilderness—the untamed, tangled part of life that frightens, yet beckons!

The dictionary defines wilderness as

(1) any unsettled, uncultivated region left in its natural condition, especially a large wild tract of land covered with dense vegetation or forest; an extensive area that is barren and empty; a waste.

(2) something likened to a wild region in bewildering vastness, perilousness, an unchecked profusion.[3]

The wilderness is repeatedly encountered as a theme and a concept in the Bible. And it is seen in contrasting dimensions.

Moses reminded the Israelites that they "went through all that great and terrible wilderness. . . ."[4] Moses described the *place* and the *experiences* of the past forty years of the Hebrew people as a wilderness. It was a wilderness physically
>   emotionally and
>   spiritually
as the Children of Israel encountered a vast wasteland in themselves. In that same passage Moses challenged the people, "Go up, take possession, as the Lord . . . has told you."[5] He was encouraging them not to be afraid of the wilderness experience or dismayed by it. Rather, they were to inherit what was intended for them
as benefits and results of the wilderness
  not instead of the wilderness!
This is a reality we must not overlook. Though we at times, like Job of old, "wander in a pathless waste"[6]—a wilderness where there is no way—we do not recognize that it is our going *through the wilderness* that enables us to experience all God has intended for us.

God allows His children to walk through dark valleys and to journey through the wilderness. The scars we encounter result in our lives being more fruitful for Him

more sensitive to Him

more obedient to Him

more loyal to Him.

While God does not inflict scars upon us to make us grow as He desires, He does promise to be with us wherever we go, giving us His grace gifts to find strength in our wilderness experiences and come out on the other side stronger and more of whom He created us to be.

Jeremiah spoke of the wilderness as a good place—a place to escape from evil and lies.[7] Isaiah prophesied about the coming time when the wilderness and dry land would rejoice.[8] Isaiah mentioned later that God would make the wilderness like Eden

the desert like a garden and it would bring forth

joy, gladness, thanksgiving, and the voice of song.[9]

"A voice cries:

In the wilderness prepare the way of the Lord,

make straight in the desert a highway for our God."[10]

The Word from God through Isaiah calls us to grasp the truth that God's road is *in* the wilderness! It is the deserted, desolate, wild regions of life where pathways of the Lord are constructed. The wilderness is where God is

where God meets us and

where God is clearing the underbrush for us

if we do not become so disheartened we cannot perceive it!

Isaiah goes on to describe how God transforms the wilderness:

"Every valley shall be lifted up,

and every mountain and hill be made low;

the uneven ground shall become level,

and the rough places a plain."

God's wilderness transformation comes through His power to reveal His glory to those with eyes to see.

After the unequaled roll call of the faithful in Hebrews 11, the writer concluded the chapter by giving a description of those who suffered abuse for God's sake:

Some were tortured, refusing to accept release, that they
might rise again to a better life. Others suffered mocking and
scourging, and even chains and imprisonment. They were
stoned, they were sawn in two, they were killed with the
sword; they went about in skins of sheep and goats, destitute,
afflicted, ill-treated—of whom the world was not worthy—
wandering over deserts and mountains and in dens and caves
of the earth (vv. 36-38).

The clear point is that God's faithful ones have always wan-
dered in the wilderness of man's rejection of God. The world
is not worthy of those who are obedient and faithful to Him.
Though living in the wilderness they survive it because their
God is the One who provides His own shelter in the deep
recesses of relationship with Him.

The wilderness is an experience of contrasts.
It is an unsettled, barren, perilous area but
    it is also a place where God is!
It is a difficult, lonely, unnerving site but
    it is also a place where God dwells!
It is a draining, exhausting, discouraging situation but
    it is also a place where God heals and strengthens!
It is a remote, desolate, debilitating condition but
    it is also a place where God moves and loves!
The shadows and darkness of the wilderness we do not seek
for ourselves, but we need not fear to advance on our wilder-
ness journey. God is there! He goes before us!
                        He comes behind us!
                        He journeys beside us!
                        He dwells within us!
Therefore we need not fear the wilderness, for there are fruits
to be born from the scars
            the wounds
                the lessons
                    the disciplines
                        the discoveries
on the wilderness with God.

The kinds of wilderness experiences are as varied as people.

Some wander in the wilderness due to their own mismanagement—they simply make bad choices.

Some struggle in the wilderness at the hands of others who are forces of evil and destruction.

Some stray in the wilderness because of the lack of meaning in their lives.

Others meander in the wilderness because of the burden of grief they bear.

Some roam in the wilderness due to the feeling of rejection by others.

Others digress in the wilderness because of the abuse and neglect they experience.

Some ramble in the wilderness because of the devastating loneliness in their lives.

I do not know the dimensions of your wilderness. I only know what mine has looked like. But because I have been there, I share with you hope and some signposts I have discovered along the way that helped me meet God there.

I have been on the journey for a long while and though the difficulties have been immense, I now can see that

the uneven ground can become level and

the rough places can become a plain.

It is my prayer that such a discovery will be yours as well. So, go forth, brothers and sisters, in the Father's name and sustaining grace. Others are journeying also!

ROBERT W. BAILEY
Birmingham, Alabama

The Crisis of the Wilderness

Aloneness
   Emptiness
     Futility
       Hopelessness
        Despair.
These feelings well up in all of us
creating crisis often blocking our efforts to grow in Christ.

Jesus experienced a crisis at the outset of His ministry
   when He spent time alone with God in the wilderness.
Christ's victory in the wilderness was monumental
   and offers us an example
               inspiration
                   direction and
                 hope.

We must decide to expose ourselves to the wilderness and
            to overcome the crisis we encounter there.

1

Crisis in the Wilderness

Dale Evans Rogers tells about a train trip which was planned for her when she was nearly four years old. She was to visit her aunts and grandfather in a Texas town 300 miles from her home. Her father had arranged with the railroad company to have the passenger train make an unscheduled stop when it came by their little station. Dale's aunt, who was a college student on her way home, would reach from the last passenger car and take little Dale from her father's arms just as the train rolled to a momentary halt.

Dale and her father arrived at the station early and waited for the train to come into sight. Dressed in her Sunday best, Dale was bubbling over with excitement as the train slowed beside them—but for some unexplained reason, just as her aunt's car came up in front of them, the train began to resume speed! There was no way her father could safely pass her to her aunt, so right in front of their eyes the train and her aunt sped off without her!

Dale cried almost all night, crying only as a disappointed child can. By morning her parents had made arrangements for her father to take her on the next train to her relatives. What had been such keen disappointment the day before now afforded her an extra treat—she would have her father all to herself for the 300-mile trip! Through her father's attentive listening and loving care, her hurt was healed, and she received a greater joy than she had anticipated.[1]

All of us have experienced times of deep hurt
                    sorrowful lamentation
            bitter despair and
                    overwhelming circumstances that press us down.
We know what it is to feel disappointment and walk in the
valley of the shadow. We know what it is to long for release
from the burdens and agony of overwhelming odds. We want
someone to make things right
            correct mistakes
        redo miscalculations.
We feel so oppressed in the thickets of life and long for a path
out, a trail through, the shadowy wilderness.

To the first-century Jew, the wilderness had a double
meaning. On the one hand it was
    a bad place
    a place where demons dwelt
    a place of temptation
    a place of testing.
On the other hand the wilderness was a place where Abraham
                                    Moses
                            prophets
                        the nation Israel and others
went to escape the world's pressures and evil, and there meet
God for special, intimate fellowship. In the process of that encounter with God came rich growth and unusual spiritual
strength. Herod the Great built his mountaintop retreat city, Ma-
sada, in the middle of the Judean desert as a place of escape
from his enemies. It is ironic that the wilderness was viewed in
such extremely opposite ways. Perhaps that was true because
    either one met God there in a life-changing way
    or one was overpowered by evil and gave up.
Jesus had many wilderness experiences: the wilderness of
being misunderstood
        rejected
        betrayed
        ridiculed.
His brief ministry began with a critical, dramatic wilderness

experience where He encountered Satan's temptation and wrestled mightily with the forces of evil. Dr. Frank Stagg wrote about Jesus' wilderness temptations (see Matt. 3:13—4:11):

> It is significant that the temptations came immediately after the baptism of Jesus. At His baptism the heavens were opened, the Spirit came, and a voice was heard to declare Him to be God's beloved Son in whom He was well pleased (3:16f). A higher moment of exhaltation can hardly be imagined. The assaults upon His will followed soon after. Moments of great vision and exaltation are precisely those in which one is most subject to such assault. The higher life is keyed to the potentiality for truth and good, the more open it is to temptation.[2]

At the outset of His ministry Jesus was compelled to make the choice of the way He would take—
for personal impulse and public expectation or
in obedience to the will of His Heavenly Father.

Mark and Luke also mention the wilderness crisis. Mark 1:12-13 simply states Jesus was in the wilderness forty days and was tempted by Satan. Luke 4:1-13 is similar to Matthew 4 with the exception of a different order of the last two temptations. Matthew's order is significant because, with his thorough emphasis on the kingdom of God, the climactic temptation is the one dealing with which kingdom one will serve.

As we recall Jesus' wilderness crisis, we must internalize that His temptations were assaults on Him not only because He faced the heavy demands of servanthood but also because His temptations, like all temptations, had a definite attractiveness. There were elements of attractiveness in His temptations, so Jesus had to determine if the end Satan proposed justified the shortcut means he offered. Few of us today stop to evaluate whether our seemingly good, attractive ends justify questionable means—we tend to submit to our temptations, relieved we can point to something we define as good!

Jesus' first temptation came after forty days of fasting and aloneness with God. Matthew tells us that Jesus was hungry. Satan pointed to the stones everywhere that were similar to the little individual loaves of bread common to Jewish daily life and challenged Jesus: "If you are the Son of God, command these stones to become loaves of bread."[3]

Jesus was hungry, and so were many people in Israel. While man does not live by bread alone, neither does he live without it! The people of Israel were looking for and desperately needing a leader who would care for them and release them from the "blind guides" who had paralyzed their spiritual vision. Jesus was tempted

not only to care for Himself

but also to provide for the hunger of His people.

He resisted the temptation with a quotation from Deuteronomy 8:3, "Man shall not live by bread alone, but by every word that proceeds from the mouth of God."

Jesus realized the people wanted bread, with or without God's Word. Jesus understood He must give them God's Word with or without bread, for the Bread of Life issues from God!

Satan then tempted Jesus by taking Him to the pinnacle of the Temple and urging Him to throw Himself down, allowing God's angels to save Him. When Satan said, "*If* You are the Son of God,"[4] he was not questioning or raising doubt about that Sonship. The Greek construction literally means, "*Since* You are the Son of God" take advantage of Your connection! The people demanded "signs and wonders." The tradition dating from the time of the prophet Malachi was that the Messiah would appear in a dramatic way at the Temple.[5] Satan was challenging Jesus to make a sensational use of God on His behalf and to draw people unto Himself. In essence, Satan was telling Jesus to take advantage of His connections to force God's protective hand for Him! But Jesus knew that such a leap would not be one of faith but of cheap manipulation. The second temptation was resisted as Jesus quoted Deuteronomy 6:16, "You shall not tempt the Lord your God."

Plant this thought deeply in your hearts and minds—*Satan used Scripture to tempt Jesus!* He quoted from Psalm 91:11-12 in his effort to coerce Jesus into following him instead of God. *Just because someone quotes Scripture does not mean they are right!* We must not forget this fact! Now that we see the devil himself cites Scripture for His advantage, we must take care that we do not allow anyone to take an isolated verse as a proof text to convince us to follow their way and not God's! The Bible can be abused to serve many views that are foreign to and far from God! In our wilderness experiences we must rely on a solid understanding of the Word of God, so we will not be detoured by false teaching or improper interpretation. While in the wilderness, one's vulnerability to lies and innuendo is great. Caution must be taken to keep the lines of communication between onself and God open during the times of pressure and stress.

The third temptation Satan posed[6] was that he would give Jesus control of all the kingdoms of the world if Jesus would worship him. This temptation is a sobering reminder that temptations at their base are false and empty! The world was not Satan's to give! He was offering a false promise in his effort to gain Jesus' indebtedness to him. Clearly the Israelites expected the Messiah to free Israel from the Roman rule and gain control over many nations. The Zealots pushed for that rule during Jesus' day and fought two bloody wars against the Romans during the next century. If Jesus had chosen to take a shortcut and succumb to Satan's temptation, He would have immediately won the hearts of the Israelites. But Jesus refused to equate the kingdom of God with the kingdom of Israel! Jesus never said His land was God's Holy Land, no more than any person in the world or the United States should say that today! Jesus resisted this final temptation telling Satan "Begone!" citing Deuteronomy 6:13,

"You shall worship the Lord your God and Him only shall you serve."

It is important for us to remember that to Jesus, who refused to bow to Satan to grasp earthly rule, was given "all power in heaven and on earth."[7] Dr. Stagg explains, "To the one who refused to seek the kingdoms of the world was given 'the kingdom of the world.'"[8]

Jesus gave an important insight to us as He lived through His wilderness crisis. So many religious hucksters today are advertising their goods with the promise of personal advantage. But all the while they shout, "Make God your copilot," they are ignoring the plans God has for each of us![9] Rather than showing us how to manipulate God

coerce God or

make God our copilot

Jesus was showing us a dependence on God and revealing to us that God is not just in the places of ease,

but He is also in the dark places!

Bill and Carolyn Self have written out of some of their own dark places to underscore how God's presence appears to His people who are sensitive and open to Him.

> It is overwhelming for us to come into some very difficult places in life, because they seem to be so dark. You think that because life has become dark, God has abandoned you. *But it is in the cloud of life that God is most vivid. It is in the deep places, the hard, difficult, agonizing places of life, where God walks the strongest* [italics mine] . . . In our pilgrimage, all along the way, God is there in the dark places. Your eyes show the burdens you carry, the crises you are up against. Your heart is aching beneath all the smooth-polished exterior you show. Most people carry a broken heart around, but we know out of the experience of our own lives that God is in the dark clouds. You can know that He is true and faithful. . . .[10]

A great Spanish mystic captured this truth in writing centuries ago:

> The soul makes greatest progress when it least thinks so, yes, most frequently when it thinks it is losing ground. The soul makes greatest progress when it travels in the dark, not knowing the way.[11]

How true this is when we realize that God is in the darkness with us—and that we do not travel alone! Yet is it not amazing how we seek to avoid all darkness? Dale Rogers has lived her faith with this conviction:

"One of the great paradoxes of the Christian faith is that we learn through difficulties and hard times. Yet we resist them in our passion to live safely and avoid hurt."[12]

If the wilderness crisis was a learning experience for our Lord and can be for us, then we need to understand how we can grow through our wilderness crises today. Dr. and Mrs. Self relate crossing the desert of the Sinai Peninsula on their way to Mount Sinai. On their second trip they took a group, many of whom became uncomfortable in that remote, isolated desert region. They traveled on the dried-up river bed which could flood immediately with only a little rain. Some of their group became fretful and ill at ease—not unlike those traveling with Moses long ago! They added this painful, beautiful insight:

> The bleakness, the beauty, the vastness, and even the mystery were somehow familiar to us. You see, we've traveled the deserts of life; we've been on the backside of God's mountain. It was familiar territory to us, because we had walked other raw landscapes in our lives. As God had used the desert experience to mature a nation, God uses life's deserts to mature His dear ones. We had gratefully accepted, for our own lives, the promise that God gave to Moses, as recorded in Exodus 33:14: "My presence will go with you, and I will give you rest."[13]

God did not mean by "rest" a passive stagnation. He meant the relief we find after responding to a challenge and being stretched by it. In growth we become more open to receive God's good gifts to us!

Over a half-century ago the Swiss psychologist Carl Jung observed about life in the Western world:

> We have built a monumental world about us, and we have slaved for it with unequalled energy. But it is so imposing because we have spent upon the outside all that is imposing in our natures—and what we find when we look within must necessarily be as it is, shabby and insufficient.[14]

We have tried so hard to eliminate all pain and inconvenience in life that we have come to believe any pain or trouble in life is a sign of weakness
> failure or
> > displeasure of God.
But as a wise counselor once noted,

"The art of living lies not in eliminating but in growing with troubles."[15]

Rather than our seeking to withdraw from the struggle
                        avoid the wilderness
                        escape the pain
                        run from the trouble

we need to embrace the truth that we mature and gain our strength not out of the easy, good times, but out of the difficult, bad times! Far too often we are deaf and blind to God's presence in our grave difficulties because of our own anger, pain, self-pity, or resentment. We tend to indulge in what one has called the "if-only" syndrome. "If only" this were different or "if only" that were changed. But the fact is, we begin the growth God intends when we cease saying "if only" and realize our wilderness crises are rare opportunities for growth![16] We want growth without pain
                        maturity without effort
                    success without work
                    progress without struggle.

The truth is people desperately want to avoid and/or escape the wilderness, but in that effort often create a more barren and tangled wilderness for themselves!

One of the profound thinkers of the last century has had a significant influence on my life. Soren Kierkegaard was a Danish writer and prophet whose early life was racked with misfortune. His introverted personality was infected with the melancholy of his father's sin of suicide. He broke his engagement to marry and in the process nearly broke his will to live. For a long time he felt his only options were debauchery, suicide, or insanity. But eventually he accepted his suffering instead of running from it. He found the meaning for his life through suffering and then discovered his vocation. When his life steadied, he released his writing which was and is a beautiful witness of the power of God to take unpromising materials in a life that is a willing tool in God's hand. One of Kierkegaard's biographers wrote of him, "He found in his writing a form of worship of God, and in the exercise of his calling as a writer whose every page was composed as under the scrutiny of God, he found his healing."[17]

This might be said of us if we would make the effort to find God's healing through our wilderness crises! In order to do so we must discover the source of interference that prompts our listening to the garbled sounds of the world instead of the clear voice of God. Not long ago we were having problems with our telephone at home. When we sought to talk, we could hear other people on another line talking. Those speaking to us could not hear these other voices. When the repairman came to service our equipment he found that a wasp nest had been built on the line where it enters our house! A small obstruction, you say, but it was sufficient to cause constant interference with our hearing what was being said to us from afar! We regained a clear line only after that interference was removed! Similarly, we gain and maintain a clear line with God only when we remove the interference that so easily crowds between us and Him!

If we are going to grow through the suffering and temptations of our wilderness crises, we must learn to pay attention to God who is still in the darkness about us. In his darkness and loneliness of persecution and imprisonment at the hands of the Nazis, Dietrich Bonhoeffer wrote these longing words to God:

> Who am I? This or the other?
> Am I one person today and tomorrow another?
> Am I both at once? A hypocrite before others
> And before myself a contemptible woe-begone weakling?
> Or is something with me still like a beaten army,
> Fleeing in disorder from a victory already achieved,
> Who am I? They mocked me these lonely questions of mine.
> Whoever I am, Thou knowest, O God, I am Thine.[18]

The deep question Bonhoeffer was asking was not just "Who am I?" but also "*Whose* am I?" He grew sufficiently in his wilderness crises to be able to affirm boldly that he belonged to God! Though the outer darkness of wilderness never subsided for Bonhoeffer, in the interior of his life there was purpose and meaning. He had journeyed through the wilderness spiritually though the physical wilderness ended only on the gallows.

These same questions keep plaguing people without and within the church today.

Who am I?

Whose am I?

Where do I belong?

To whom do I belong?

There are so many attempts to acquire artificial answers to these questions. People flock to join a gang

a group

a club

a civic function

a secret society

a fraternity

a sorority

a political party

a religion

even a church

all in an effort to conceal their longing to escape their anxiety and avoid the pain of their wilderness crises! People yearn for company and multitudes, while the truth is: the wilderness experience is actually a very solitary thing.

We point indicting fingers at those today who search for artificial means to deal with their inner hunger and thirst, yet we must ask if the wilderness experience meant anything to those Israelite leaders who appeared the closest to God? Did it have significant carryover? Exodus 24 tells us that Aaron, his two sons, and seventy of the elders of Israel went with Moses part of the way up Mount Sinai, and there they saw God! (v. 11). It was a glorious encounter of rich fellowship! While Joshua went with Moses further up the mountain, Moses left Aaron in charge of all who remained behind.

Then we read in Exodus 32 that the people grew weary of how long it took Moses to receive God's Word. So they went to Aaron—as Moses instructed if they had a question—and when they asked him to make them gods, Aaron gave the instructions for the idol construction! Remember: Aaron had only recently seen God and partaken of a covenant meal in response to that privileged encounter! But as soon as the power and pressure of the people came upon him, Aaron forgot the strength and resolve that had come during the holy moment and entered into a forsaken wilderness of idolatry, rebellion, and sin!

Aaron, influenced by those who had not seen God and who wanted "instant religion and a quick spiritual high," entered into a self-made wilderness and took with him many others. Aaron did not allow the assurance of God's presence and power to linger with him to strengthen his will and sharpen his spiritual commitment. Aaron did not trust God enough when he could not plainly see the paths in the wilderness. As a result, he sinned and traveled into the barren remoteness far from God.

Four years ago on a staff retreat at the outset of one of the darkest years of my life, I discovered this prayer of Thomas Merton, one of the most influential Christians of the last half century. He became a Christian as an adult and soon entered the Trappist Monastery in Kentucky where he lived and wrote for nearly 35 years. He prayed:

> My Lord God,
> I have no idea where I am going.
> I do not see the road ahead of me.
> I cannot know for certain where it will end.
> Nor do I really know myself,
> and the fact that I think
> that I am following your will
> does not mean that I am actually doing so.
> But I believe that the desire to please you
> does in fact please you.
> And I hope that I have that desire
> in all that I am doing.
> I hope that I will never do anything
> apart from that desire.
> And I know that if I do this
> you will lead me by the right road
> though I may know nothing about it.
>
> Therefore will I trust you always
> though I may seem to be lost

and in the shadow of death.
I will not fear, for you are ever with me,
and will never leave me to face my perils alone.[19]

Merton was echoing the psalmist who, too, had walked
through the valley of the shadows and could affirm to God,
"Thou art with me!"

There is a part of Matthew 4, we may often overlook.
"Then the devil left him, and behold, angels came and ministered to him."[20]

In the aftermath of the wilderness fast and temptations,
ministering angels came to Jesus. What a beautiful picture of
blessed encouragement and compassionate love! Have you
ever considered who might those angels be for the wilderness
crises in our lives, as well as in the lives of those about us?
Friends may be the angels God sends to others! But if we en-
gage in the ministry of angels, we must be open and receptive
to be God's comforters to the hurting hearts surrounding us.
Dale Rogers writes:

> ". . . there is another healer for this hard time in our lives—
> we can be sensitive to the needs of those around us and offer
> ourselves and our services to people who are sorely in need
> of a friend. And in spite of the facades that people wear,
> there is an almost universal longing on their part for someone
> to listen to them, to talk with them, and share in their hurts
> and anxieties. *Our loneliness, when harnessed to helpfulness,
> can be a tremendous blessing to someone else*[21] (italics mine).

We can cope with our wilderness crises and discover
growth in our dark places when we
  forget ourselves in God's service
  experience the transforming power of God and
  learn to listen to God and to others.
We can free ourselves from a great deal of the undesirable
sense of abandonment of the wilderness when we share com-
passionately with fellow travelers and when we receive openly
those who share with us. Bill and Carolyn Self acknowledge:

Only a person who has walked a similar road can understand the raw suffering, the throbbing pain in the inner being; only a fellow traveler can comprehend the torment of anger, grief, and shame that is a part of the human reaction to pain. One of God's most generous gifts to us is the gift of friends, those who can support and walk with us through a situation. Not only do we enjoy this gift for ourselves, but we can, in turn, be that support for someone else. This is God incarnate.[22]

God in Jesus Christ has shown us how to deal properly with our wilderness crises and make ourselves open to growth through pain and suffering. The decision is left to each reader whether to

be overwhelmed by your wilderness experiences or

grow through the darkness of your wilderness experiences. Jesus endured and overcame the evil of His negative wilderness experiences and He often enjoyed the quiet rest of His positive wilderness experiences. We must learn the contrasts and potential of the wilderness!

Either we will waste all of God's presence and power in the wilderness crises of our lives, or we will learn from Jesus' experience how we are to live in harmony and union with God. A devout Christian of centuries ago wrote:

The highest perfection does not consist in interior joys, nor in sublime raptures, nor in visions, nor in having the gift of prophecy, but in bringing our will into such conformity with the will of God that whatever we know He desires, that also shall we desire with our whole affection.[23]

The encouragement given you is that you approach cautiously your wilderness experiences so you can overcome their crises and doing the will of God. To do less is to waste their potential. To desire to do the will of God is Christ's intent for all His disciples. Usually we understand this truth only after a wilderness crisis!

The Trap of Wrong Answers

Temptation.
Everyone experiences it.
Few ask the right questions about it.
Some feel guilty about it.
Many quickly succumb to it.

Temptation.
Who will you love?
How will you spend your time?
What values will you hold?
To whom will you give your allegiance?

Temptation.
Life is full of questions and
    there are answer-givers everywhere.
Accepting the wrong answers for these questions
    constructs a trap of great pain and problems.
Wrongdoing comes not from confronting temptation
    but in dealing with it improperly.

Temptation.
Do you recognize it when you face it?
What is your answer for it?
How do you deal with it?
Can you avoid the trap of wrong answers?

2

The Trap of Wrong Answers

The question of God and His relationship to man has been a critical question since the beginning of time. A great deal of the effort of many people's lives is spent trying to discover how to coerce
    manipulate
      convince or
        ignore God.
On the other hand people are devoting time seeking to find
                      hear
                    understand
                obey God.
Marcellus, a soldier in the monumental novel, *The Robe*, wrote to Diana, the woman he loved who lived in Rome. After he had described to her his conversation with Jesus of Nazareth, she quickly wrote him in reply, "What I feared was that it might somehow affect your life—and mine, too. It is a beautiful story, Marcellus, a beautiful story. Let it remain so. We don't have to understand it. And we don't have to do anything about it, do we?"[1]

The answer Diana reached was one that fills the minds of multitudes of people today. The story of God's redemptive love in Jesus Christ is a "beautiful story"—*but we do not have to do anything about it, do we?* When we reach or echo such a conclusion, we are clearly offering the wrong answer to the most vital question of life! And to keep on giving and living the

wrong answers to life's most important questions is only to
wind up with a life of pain
                              guilt
                            isolation
                          frustration
                        anxiety and
                        alienation!
We are susceptible to temptation when we go through the
tangled maze of life. We are enticed by the temptations
of easy escape from sin
    of no lasting consequences for our actions
        of instant pleasure
            of endless power.
    A Desert Father centuries ago described the life of one
who knows the right answers and walks with God. He said
the characteristics of a follower are that one loves the Lord
and hates evil and determines

    not to walk in agreement with an unjust man,
    not to look with his eyes upon evil,
    nor to go about being curious,
    and neither to examine nor to listen to the business of others.
    Not to take anything with his hands,
        but rather to give to others.
    Not to be proud in his heart,
    nor to malign others in his thoughts.
    Not to fill his stomach,
        but in all things to behave with discretion.[2]

From this kind of contemplative devotion obedience to God
comes. The refusal to follow those who are evil and do what
is evil enables our fellowship with God to grow. Avoiding com-
plaining and downgrading others, while at the same time leaving the company of those who assassinate the character of
others, allows the fellowship of Christ to develop.
    Throughout the generations of mankind, from the first to
this one, our biggest problem has
    not been knowing what was right
    but being willing to do what we knew was right!

The reason why so many have fallen to temptation is
   not because they did not realize they were being tempted
but because they failed to resist the temptation!
The sin lies not in the temptation
                  but in dwelling upon the tempting thought
                  and in doing what we are tempted to do!
A young man once went to his spiritual leader with an uneasy
anxiety about the temptations which arose in his mind. The
wise man told him to take off his coat and catch the wind in it.
The young man replied that he could not catch the wind! The
wise leader concluded, "If you cannot catch the wind, neither
can you prevent distracting thoughts from coming into your
head. Your job is to say 'No' to them."[3]

   And each of us does have the ability to say "No" to temptation when we are willing to exercise that capability. Yet too
often we choose the wrong answer to the question of temptation and justify our lust
                  condone our envy
                  defend our jealousy
                  rationalize our hatred
                  excuse our greed
                  soft-pedal our gossip
                  whitewash our destructiveness
                  alibi our wrongdoing.

   What a tragic picture Genesis 3 paints of the trap of wrong
answers! God had just finished His creation and placed Adam
in charge of it all. God created a woman for Adam, and
Adam was so excited about having a companion like he was
that he could not think of a name for her—though he had
given a name to every bird and animal![4] Unable to think of a
name, Adam called his mate literally, "Part of me. Woman,
because she was taken out of Man."[5] And thus the man and
the woman were together in the perfect Garden which had
everything they needed. They had the possibility of continual
life there in the presence and fellowship of God.

   Into the Garden came a gatecrasher—a serpent, which
evidently walked upright and wanted entry into the Garden

rather than life in the wild. The serpent went to the Woman who had heard second-hand that they were to enjoy everything in the Garden with the exception of the Tree of Knowledge in the middle of the Garden. In a clever and cunning manner, the serpent appeared to be the woman's friend and helper when he questioned literally in the Hebrew, "Has God really said . . . ?" "Did God actually say . . . ?" "So it is the case that God said, 'You shall not eat of the fruit of the trees of the garden'?"[6]

The woman corrected the tempter by saying they were permitted to eat of all the trees except one, lest they die. The serpent then lied about God twice.

- He said they would not die if they ate from the forbidden tree.
- Furthermore, the serpent said if they did eat that fruit the Man and the Woman would become like God—knowing everything He knew!

"So when the woman saw that the tree was good for food,
                and that it was a delight to the eyes,
            and that the tree was desired to make one wise,
        she took of its fruit and ate;
    and she also gave some to her husband,
                and he ate."[7]

The result of their eating was a sense of shame and guilt before God! They knew they had done wrong, but now they felt trapped by their wrong answer to the tempter's question! The fact we must never forget is that

one wrong answer to the Deceiver leads to another
one lie necessitates another to cover it up
one deceitful act requires another to conceal it
one hate-filled plot demands another to complete it
one slanderous slur precipitates another to support it
one prejudiced choice enables another to succeed it
one ungodly attitude propels another to endorse it!

The guilt Adam and Eve felt for their sin was so great they could not look each other in the eye!

They hid from each other with clothing hurriedly made and
they hid themselves from God.
You know the feeling they had! You know the times you have
felt cutting guilt within you. And you know when you have
looked at a person whose eyes were always shifting and looking away from you because of the guilt of the sin in their evil
hearts!

The drama moved quickly. The serpent tempted the
Woman, who in turn tempted the Man—and they both
sinned! Then God questioned Man about what he had done.
Understand clearly that God does not need for us to inform
Him about our thoughts and deeds—He already knows them!
But what God did was have the Man convict himself out of his
own mouth! And the interrogation ended with
the Woman blaming the serpent and
the Man blaming the Woman *and* God for his sin!

After all, the man said, "The woman whom thou gavest to
be with me, she gave me fruit of the tree, and I ate."[8] Suc-
cumbing to the temptation led to an arrogance of blame and
self-protection. Because they built their trap with their first
wrong answers to the tempter, now each had to live with the
outgrowth of that trap.
The serpent was cursed and made to crawl.
The Woman was punished with pain.
The Man was punished with more difficult work.
They both were expelled from the Garden!
At this point there is frequently some unfortunate confusion.
God did not curse the Man and the Woman.
Work was not their punishment—they were already working
in the garden.
But now their work would be harder, and they were ex-
pelled from the Garden of Life.
As they were preparing to leave their comfortable home,
Adam named his wife Eve, which literally means "Life." Earlier
he could only call her "part of me," but now he named her his
partner in their new venture of life.[9]

Thus the story of Adam and Eve has become the story of every person. Over the generations we have repeatedly given our wrong answers to the questions of the tempter, and thus we have created our traps of guilt and sin! If we are to understand temptation fully, we must keep in view two important facts. *One is that we have the greatest tendency to sin when we reach a peak in our lives.*

When we think we have it all
When we feel we have arrived
When we believe others are following us
When we conclude that only we are right
When we decide that we are in charge
When we assume that we have great power
When we deduce that we have achieved our goal
When we presume that we are above sin

these are the times when we are most susceptible to falling into temptation! When we feel the strongest is when we become the weakest! When we think we are invincible we expose ourselves most completely to the tempter. When we decide that one point of agreement with the tempter will not compromise our position is when we fall flat on our face!

The second fact of temptation is that we are not tempted by God! Adam blamed God for his temptation. We have heard countless people claim that

God placed the temptation in front of them
God cast the burden upon them
God predetermined their course of action for them
God seduced them with the glamor of the temptation.

But God's Word says that God does not tempt any person! The reason God created you is not merely in order that He could have some amusement in tempting you to deny Him and destroy yourself! James wrote this truth clearly in 1:13-15:

Let no one say when he is tempted,
"I am tempted by God,"
for God cannot be tempted with evil
and he himself tempts no one [italics mine];
but each person is tempted when he is

lured and enticed by his own desire.
Then desire when it has conceived gives birth to sin;
and sin when it is full-grown brings forth death.

Make no mistake—*God does not tempt you!* You are not a puppet He plays with and then delights when you fall! Paul described God's action in regard to temptation so clearly in 1 Corinthians 10:13, "God is faithful, and *he will not let you be tempted* beyond your strength, but with the temptation will also provide the way of escape, that you may be able to endure it."

Paul did not say God will not allow His faithful ones to be tempted. Paul did affirm that God will not allow any of His children to be tempted beyond their endurance and that God will provide a means to escape the temptation if we are willing to accept it! Implant these three points deeply in your mind:
God does not tempt you
God does not allow anyone to be tempted beyond your
    strength to resist and
God provides you a way to escape the temptation!
He may allow us to go into the wilderness and struggle through the wilderness, but God does not tempt us in the wilderness!

Sometimes it is only when we are courageous enough to venture forth in the world's wilderness that we discover the strength, power, and presence of God. Two decades ago Samuel Miller wrote,

> There comes a time when a man, to be man, must move beyond safety, beyond the easy conformities, beyond self-assurance, into the turmoil and terror of life lived heroically. If a man wants eternal life, it is to be found only at a risk, only where one pushes out into deep water. Insecurity is the name of the Christian's daring, of his faith, and ultimately of his peace in God.[10]

Surely that time has come for us to move beyond safety and easy conformities into the flow of life in which there is risk and uncertainty. But the tempter keeps asking us

if God really said we are to take a risk
if God really wants us going into deep water
if God really intends us to experience insecurity.
And every time we give the wrong answer to temptation, we
bury ourselves even deeper in the trap of our own sin!

One of the Desert Fathers who had a complete copy of the
Bible on fine parchment met a man who was trapped with his
wrong answers to temptation. The man came to visit the spiritual leader and stole the valuable Bible. When the devoted
Christian realized the man had robbed him, he spoke not a
word for fear he would cause the man to lie as well as steal.
The robber took the book to a nearby city to sell it. The pro-
spective buyer said he would need to borrow the book to have
it appraised. He carried it to the original owner, knowing that
he had a valuable Bible, and asked if it were worth what the
seller was asking for it. The humble Desert Father replied that
it was a fine book and worth the asking price. The merchant
then returned to the robber and told him the Desert Father
had agreed it was worth the price, and so the merchant decided the buy the book.

The robber became very anxious and asked if the old
Christian had said anything else. When the merchant replied
that he had not, the robber suddenly informed the merchant
he had changed his mind and could not sell the book. He
then hurried back to the Desert Father and begged him to take
back the book. From the negative wilderness of temptation
that resulted in the theft of the book, the robber moved into
the positive wilderness of the realization of his wrong—of coming to himself and of committing himself to God and His servant. The devout Christian refused to take back the Bible,
saying he was making it a present to his robber. The bewil-
dered thief then responded, "If you do not take it back, I shall
never have any peace."[11]

The recorder of this episode concludes that the thief stayed
with that Desert Father for the rest of his life! He had trapped
himself with his wrong answer to the temptation

of getting something dishonestly
  of obtaining something for nothing
    of acquiring something selfishly
and so he wound up indebted to his benefactor for life! His
stay was for his own benefit—not as punishment or a conse-
quence of succumbing to temptation. It was a positive act of a
repentant heart.

We are living in an age when more and more people are
giving the wrong answers to temptation. Never have there
been so many people who claim to deserve something for
nothing or who claim they deserve more than they invested.

Two attitudes and practices of our day are quite alarm-
ing. One is the pyramid scheme of getting rich quickly and
easily. The scheme is similar to the chain letter that has been
outlawed. The only difference is that a product is being sold
and people work for the ones at the top of the pyramid. But
the intent is basically the same. For little or no work, a person
is sometimes able to become rich. He does so not because he
has used his mind, his hands, or his life to help others, but
because he has manipulated others through a conspiracy in
which a few people at the top get rich on the energy and efforts of a large number of workers below them.

The second practice is even more subtle and painful than
the pyramid scheme, for herein people plan to get more than
they have rightfully invested. Whether it is

                industry or insurance
                securities or commodities
                employer or government
the attitude of a growing segment of our population is that
"'big government' or 'big business' owes me something"—
whether or not those persons have invested themselves or
their money in the agency that pays the bill! Few people seem
to understand—or care—that the dividends paid out to Social
Security recipients in the 1970s and 1980s in no way resem-
ble the contributions made by the worker before retirement.
While the original genius of this program was to help those in

a financial crisis, now the middle and upper income people seem to be gaining greater benefits through Social Security than the poor. In each strata of society the common attitude is that the recipient feels he deserves to get all he can, regardless of whether or not he has paid anything or the full amount into Social Security.

That was not the reaction of one Chinese family. It was 1980 when Vietnamese refugees were still trying to enter America. A former colonel in Chiang Kai Shek's army came to America in the late 1970s and set as his goal getting all of his family to America. By December of 1980 he had almost succeeded in the long trek for his family members who had left China for Vietnam years before, and now were escaping Vietnam and coming to America. When that father of two grown children who had come to America died suddenly, his children went to make arrangements for the funeral. The funeral director explained they could apply for and receive $255 from Social Security for funeral expenses. But those children said he had not paid anything into Social Security, and they would not take anything from it. They paid for his funeral by themselves! They did something for America that most Americans fail to do for one another! They refused to take from "big government" what had not been earned by their family!

If our nation is to have financial integrity, and if Christian people are to have inner vitality we must learn to resist the wrong answers to difficult questions and quit expecting from others something we do not deserve or have not earned. Clearly the reason the state lotteries are so popular and profitable for states across the land is because people continue to attempt to get something for nothing—to get an astronomical return for a one-dollar investment! Without a doubt, it will take insight and courage for us to resist the voice of the tempter and wean ourselves away from expecting something for nothing. The late Carlyle Marney hit the nail on the head when he observed that the principal work of the church today is the recovery of courage. The church that has lost its drawing power

                                    its stature
                               its station and
                               its influence
is the church that has lost its courage and heart for the task to
which Christ has called it! We will inevitably be smothered in
an ever-tightening trap when we succumb to the tempter and
seek to live with wrong answers!

   How often we are tempted to give up

                          to give in
                     to follow the crowd!
Less than sixty days before his tragic, fatal plane crash, U.N.
Secretary General Dag Hammarskjold wrote about his life:

> Tired
> And lonely,
> So tired
> The heart aches.
> Meltwater trickles
> Down the rocks,
> The fingers are numb,
> The knees tremble.
> It is now,
> Now, that you must not give in.
>
> On the path of the others
> Are resting places
> Places in the sun
> Where they can meet.
> But this
> Is your path
> And it is now,
> Now, that you must not fail.
>
> Weep
> If you can,
> Weep
> But do not complain,
> The way chose you—
> And you must be thankful. [12]

It is all right to weep in our struggle with the tempter, but we must never complain, for this is our lot when we make the choice to become a follower after Jesus Christ our Lord!

Clearly a primary reason why so many people today continue to be trapped with wrong answers to their difficult questions is that they do not know the meaning and purpose of their lives! When we assume that we deserve to be happy
we are supposed to be happy
we work hard enough to be happy
then we are going to be discouraged when we are not happy! An unhappy person is always more ready to give in to the temptation that promises happiness, but Christ's followers are not called to a life of discipleship in which we experience perpetual happiness. Happiness is not the end or goal of our Christian faith—it is an outgrowth or by-product. Our purpose and goal is to know intimate fellowship with God in Christ Jesus and to serve Him as we live out His love! Phillips paraphrased Ephesians 5:15, "Live life then, with a due sense of responsibility, not as men who do not know the meaning and purpose of life, but as those who do."

When we know in Christ our meaning and purpose in life,
we will never have quick and easy answers nor
will we always have easy circumstances in life.
We will weep and struggle just as did our Lord, but we will know that we are not alone in that process. And the gift of Christ is the "peace that surpasses all understanding"[13] and the inner security and joy that only He can give—and no one or nothing can take from us!

The Desert Fathers and others have warned us that following a high spiritual experience and intensive time of prayer and meditation, depression or "the dark night of the soul" often overwhelms the devoted disciple. At the time in which we might think we are the strongest—that is the very time when the temptation to give the wrong answer is the greatest! Some have characterized this feeling as dread, saying there is an overwhelming sense of unworthiness and a feeling that God does not care about you.[14] You have felt some of these moments. But remember what Jesus Christ did. Luke underscores the fact that

Jesus was led by the Spirit into the wilderness
> to grow in His communion with His Heavenly Father
> and to gain total commitment to His will.

Jesus was tempted by the devil in the wilderness
> in an effort to control His response
> and to limit His effectiveness in the world.[15]

He was hungry after His forty-day fast and meditation. Satan tempted Him to turn one of the plentiful stones from the desert into bread. Jesus replied by quoting from the Scripture which was part of His mind and life, "Man shall not live by bread alone."[16]

Moses had uttered those words to the Israelites when they were tempted to succumb to pride and self-sufficiency. Now Jesus was taking care not to give the wrong answer and fall into pride and self-sufficiency Himself! Faith in God or being a child of God is not dependent on how much one has or on some kind of magical power. On the contrary, our relationship to God is evidenced by our confident faith in the midst of life's most difficult circumstances! God taught the Israelites that man is more than stomach and he needs more than bread—mankind needs to depend on the loving care of God to provide what he needs. The same God who provided manna in the wilderness for His people firmly promises to provide for and sustain His own children! Jesus resisted the temptation to abandon such trust in God![17]

What a victory that was for our Lord!

He had emerged from His time of growing fellowship with
> the Father

He had felt His inner joy and spiritual high, and yet

He had also resisted the temptation to forget who He was
> or what He was about!

We must never forget that our Lord was tempted like as we are—by the devil

      in an attractive manner
        appealing to self-interests
          promising immediate satisfaction and pleasure
but Jesus used His God-given means to escape the temptation
and avoid giving a wrong answer! Our Lord quoted Scripture
He had committed to memory in order to resist the devil and
His first temptation. Our Savior stood firm on the public commitment He had made in the Jordan River to fulfill God's purpose in His life.

During the French Revolution, the heir apparent to the
French throne, the young Dauphin, was taken hostage by the
mobs. Those who captured him thought by temptation and
torture they could convince him to ignore and denounce his
kingship. In order to achieve their goal, they placed the young
Prince in the company of some of the foulest people in Paris
so his character might be dissipated. Much to their dismay, this
attempt was unsuccessful, because the young Prince never fell
victim to the temptation to give the wrong answer! With each
prodding to concur with the life-style and attitude of his cap-
tors, he would stomp his foot and shout, "No! No! No! I was
born to be a King!"[18]

And so are we! We are born to be kings, and only when
we assert our authentic purpose and stay true to the Holy
Spirit's leading in our lives will we avoid the trap of wrong answers of giving in to temptation which deepens.

Without question it is difficult to be on the pilgrimage of
spiritual fellowship and resist the flood of temptations all
around us. But we have the clue for how to accomplish this
worthy end. Paul has given us reassurance of our Lord's provision in 1 Corinthians 10:13 that we will have a way to escape
our temptation. We also can adopt the insight of David Living-
ston who stated how he found the staying power in the dark
lands of Africa long ago. He simply said he found his strength
from the word of the Gentleman who said—"Lo, I am with
you always, even unto the end of the world."[19]

As Jesus the Christ depended on the strength of His

Father, so we can depend on the strength of our Heavenly Father—manifested through the Holy Spirit who is always with us in the wilderness, giving us power over temptation and the means to escape the trap of wrong answers in face of the tempter. We must understand Him, and we must do something about His revelation to us.

He calls us to a holy, unique, set-apart life, all of which is possible when we respond in faithful obedience to Him rather than succumb to the trap of simplistic

self-satisfying

wrong answers to temptation!

Bargaining with God

There is a lot of bargaining going on every day.
    We bargain with others to change.
    We bargain with others to agree with us.
    We bargain with others to leave us alone.
    We bargain with others to help us.

God does not escape our bargaining schemes.
    We bargain for Him to validate our decisions.
    We bargain for Him to fulfill our wishes.
    We bargain for Him to give us security.
    We bargain for Him to settle our anxieties.

Bargaining can be wearisome and can cause distress to characterize all relationships.
We spend most of our days in weary bargaining.
    We extend much of our energy in lonely distrust.
        We may wind up with less than what we wanted
                or more than we anticipated.

What is it we want from God?
Are we willing to let Him give us His good gifts?
When will we learn to trust God?
How can we approach God without bargaining with Him?

3

Bargaining with God

In one of his fables, Aesop told of a Dog that was running along the banks of the Nile River. He was nearly overcome with thirst, but he was hesitant to stop for fear of the river monsters. Thus, as the Dog lowered his head and lapped up the water while he ran, a Crocodile raised up from the river and asked why he was in such a hurry. In a kind voice, the Crocodile said he would like the opportunity of becoming acquainted and would become a friend if only the Dog would slow down. The ferocious river animal pled a good bargain for their friendship, but the Dog concluded as he ran rapidly on, "You do me great honor, but it is to avoid such companions as you that I am in so much haste."[1]

The Dog was wise in understanding the Crocodile's bargain was one he could not afford to accept!

It seems that we cannot turn around without
either someone presenting a bargain to us
or our offering a bargain to others!
Our society has become accustomed to bargaining
whether we are buying or building
whether we are talking to a friend or to our family.
We are almost always in the shadow of a bargain in which we
are exchanging something that will benefit us for something
that will benefit another—though we hope our benefit is the
greater! Often our bargaining is taking place with those who
are evil and seek to destroy our ability

> our influence
> our energy
> our reputation.

We are not always as wise as the Dog who avoided the evil bargain of the pleasant-talking, mal-intending Crocodile!

The bargaining done in our society has not been limited between people. Frequently we witness people who are wrapped up in bargaining with God. Several years ago a patient in the hospital talked with his pastor about the impending major surgery that might not be successful. The man was angry and hostile. He told his pastor that he had decided to make a deal with God. If God would see him through that surgery and renew his health, then he promised God he would begin regular church attendance, and both he and his family would assume an active role in church. During the preceding years the pastor knew this man had been in the church's buildings less than a half-dozen times! And the long-term pattern of that church member was never more than twice a year in corporate worship.

The man underwent surgery.

The surgery was successful.

His body was cured.

His strength was soon renewed.

But the man still practices the same religious attitude! Twice-a-year church attendance is still his practice. He made a bargain with God when he felt it was to his advantage, but then as soon as the crisis was over, he went back on his word!

Several years ago there was a classic account of such bargaining with God in an airplane. While crossing the Rocky Mountains the plane encountered a storm, and the pilot warned the passengers, after a desperate struggle of several minutes, that the plane would probably crash. A wealthy passenger realized that his death might be only second away! In a flurry of prayer he bargained with God that if God would get him down safely he would never fly again. And furthermore, the man promised to give half his wealth to the church and to tithe for as long as he lived! In a miraculous manner the storm quietened, and the plane made a safe landing! As he walked off the plane the man seated next to him asked what he was going to do about the prayers he had uttered aloud during the storm. The wealthy man replied without hesitation, "Well, I don't intend to fly again soon—but I figure since the government is getting close to half of my money anyway, God won't mind if I keep what is left without giving Him any!"

Again, when the crisis was over, the bargain was voided and the man went on his way!

It is not necessary to have experienced such crises as these to have engaged in bargaining with God at some time or another in your life. You have been caught up in a time of disappointment or defeat when you felt that

you needed some sign from God

you needed some response from God

you needed some gift from God

to help you keep on trying to be and do your best. Quite often not only is the concept of bargaining wrong, but also the bargains we try to strike with God are not fair in what is expected or requested. The Jewish tradition that was written down in the Talmud describes several types of situations for which the faithful Jew is not to pray. These include

not praying for the past to be rewritten

not praying for nature to be changed and

not praying for harm to come to another.[2]

There once were two storekeepers who were bitter rivals. They watched each other across the street all day long, glaring at the successes of the other and gloating over their own gains. One night an angel appeared in a dream to one of the store owners. He told the man God wanted to teach him a lesson. God agreed to give this merchant anything he asked for, but whatever he received, his competitor across the street would get twice as much! If he wanted wealth, health, fame, or children, his request would be granted with the knowledge that his rival would receive twice what came to him! The spiteful man thought for only a moment and then asked, "All right, my request is: strike me blind in one eye!"

There are some people who have so completely sold their souls to the devil that they would be willing to suffer inconvenience if they would drive a bargain with God which would destroy their rivals! Your efforts to bargain with God may not have reached such proportions, yet perhaps you have wanted to gain from God some special concession in your job

for your family

in your studies

with your friends

by your finances.

Because of the condition in which you have suddenly found yourself, you want to bargain with God

    to solve your problems

    to increase your financial assets

    to conquer your disease

    to cease your aging process

    to avert your death

    to cure the disease of your loved one

    to heal the pain caused by your loved one's death

    to remove obstacles, disappointments in your life

    to open doors of opportunity for success.

So often you get bogged down in your self-pity that you fail to see what the Healing God offers you at the same time you are trying to manipulate from Him some solution on *your* terms.

An old Chinese legend tells about the death of a woman's 'y son. Her loss was so great that she went to the religious ler of her community and asked what rite he could offer in 'r to restore her son to life. In his wisdom he told her to go a mustard seed in a home that had not experienced sor- and that seed would be used to eliminate her sorrow. She immediately set out to find that home and came first to a mansion where she explained her quest and asked if they had ever known sorrow. The immediate response was she had come to the wrong place, for they were overwhelmed with sorrow which they recited to her. She considered who might minister to them better than she in light of the grief she had experienced with her son, so she stayed and cared for them through their time of painful heartache. Then she continued on her search for a mustard seed in a home that had known no sorrow. Everywhere she went, from the richest mansion to the poorest shack, she heard more tales of grief and woe. After a time she became so wrapped up in caring for people in their need that she forgot her original quest! Seeing and caring for the pain of others had driven the paralyzing grief from her own life![3]

We all have had or will have pain

problems

suffering

grief

in our lives. We are misguided when we approach God with a deal like—Give me . . . and I'll do for you . . .

Help me . . . and I'll do for you . . .

Do for me . . . and I'll do for you . . .

God cannot be bought! We have neither the option nor the opportunity to initiate a bargain with God, in spite of how often we try to manipulate our request from Him. We do not win God's approval nor do we change His mind when we offer Him some fantastic promise for granting our special request. God desires that we come to Him not for reward

not to escape death

but out of love for Him

love which He has given us!

Still, people continue in their bargaining efforts. The conclusion in the book, *Ministering to the Grieving,* penned several years ago, still stands: "As though one could gain a prize for

Often we tend to be like Jacob. We fall victim to the temptation that we can and may strike our bargain with God. In Genesis 28 we have a record of Jacob offering God a bargain while he was fleeing from his father and brother. Jacob had deceived his brother, Esau, with an unfair bargain. He had deceived his father, Isaac, and headed to his Uncle Laban whom he would later deceive! Jacob's life was a vast wasteland. Not only had he created an isolated wilderness for himself, but also his actions had brought a barren landscape into the lives of others. At night during that hasty journey Jacob promised God that if He would be with him

if He would bless him

if He would protect him

if He would prosper him

if He would return him to his father's house

then Jacob would worship God only and would even build an altar and give God a tithe of all he earned! Jacob seemed to feel he could manipulate God into a favorable position by his clever words and shrewd bargaining. Some twenty years after that attempt to bargain with God, Jacob approaches the same place in Genesis 32. Now he is heading back to meet his brother, Esau, whom he had tricked out of the eldest son's paternal blessing. Jacob has his wives and flocks, the full evidence of his prosperity, with him. This time he addresses God not to offer a bargain but to ask for God's help! Surely this was sign of Jacob's maturing. He did not come with conditions God to act—he merely fell before God admitting what he going to face was too big for him to handle by himself. He ed God's help! In the wilderness of his life Jacob had finally unearthed the secret to real survival: self in relationship God. The need of his tangled life suddenly was so overning that the "Trickster" could no longer rely on his cunut had to face his own weakness and need of Divine

timately this is the only way we can come before God— bargain with Him

but to ask His help
not to tell God what we will do
but to accept what God will do for us!

We need to face the fact that God is not trying to put us down by posing great tests for us and then being entertained by all those who fail life's difficult challenges. God does not abandon us after His creation of us and then sit back and watch us fall flat on our faces when we are stumped by the obstacles of life. But in love God has created us with the gift of freedom, thereby allowing us to make wise choices as well as poor ones. And most of all, God allows us to live in a world that is pricked by evil and is often quite unfair.

No matter what we do or how hard we try, God does not promise us life without pain
life without problems
life without difficulties
life without the wilderness.

God *does* tell us that through the Lordship of Jesus Christ and the presence of His Spirit He will give us the power and ability to choose what will be our response to the wilderness experiences of life. The old adage reminds us, "The same fire that melts the butter hardens the egg!"[7]

We can either come unglued in the storms of life, or we can receive God's strength and grow stronger! We can either melt in the heat and oppression of the wilderness or be fortified by the purifying processes of the wilderness experience. Our growth and maturity will come
not as a result of our bargaining with God
but as a result of God's gracious giving to us
when we are willing to receive from His hand. The same good God who gave His unique Son that we might know life abundant and eternal is the God who will give us strength

hope
courage and
patience

when all the energy and vitality seem to have been sapped
from us.

In Matthew's record of Jesus' second temptation, the devil
took Jesus up to the highest point of the Temple and urged
Him to throw Himself down so the angels might save Him.[8]
Here was the height of an attempt to bargain with God—
Satan tempting God's very Son to ask the Father to save His
life when He jumped off the highest point in Jerusalem just so
He could prove His identity! Again, Jesus resisted the devil's
temptation to abandon His Father's plan for His life by quoting
Scripture which was implanted in His mind and heart. He
replied,

"Again it is written,

'You shall not tempt the Lord your God.'"[9]

Jesus withstood the temptation to bargain with God

the temptation to disobey God

the temptation to rebel against God

the temptation to deny God

the temptation to abandon God

the temptation to distrust God

by using the power of the Spirit within Him and

by referring to the Scripture that was part of Him.

In this context we can appreciate more fully the impact of
Isaiah's declaration:

"Thou dost keep him in perfect peace,

whose mind is stayed on thee,

because he trusts in thee.

Trust in the Lord for ever,

for the Lord God

is an everlasting rock."[10]

Look closely at the components of that declaration. God
keeps in perfect peace the one

whose mind is focused on Him

because that person trusts in God, the everlasting rock!

Without a doubt, the reason many of us fret our days in

restless anxiety is that our minds are not focused on God and
we do not trust Him! Do we not wind up in many last-minute
efforts to bargain with God because we do not depend on
God's Word or the covenantal promise He has made with us?
Do we not dissipate our strength

> dilute our energy and
>
> distract our witness

by our concerted efforts to manipulate God into our way of
thinking instead of dedicating ourselves in line with His directives?

The reason why so many people are overwhelmed by
temptation is that they have courted it for so long they have
lost the ability to withstand it! Strong athletes build their diets
not on what is considered "quick energy" foods such as cook-
ies and candy, but on the durable, long-lasting foods such as
spaghetti and potatoes. In one test the runners who ate choco-
late candy quickly lost their power to resist the effort of another to push their arm down, while those who had eaten
properly and avoided the candy had their full strength. We all
will experience problems and disappointments in life. The only
way for us to avoid seeking the "quick and easy," weak answers is to develop the spiritual diet that will sustain us in our
greatest need.

A wise Desert Father pointed out that one who is following
Christ should realize that when evil thoughts raised by the
devil confront him he should fly by prayer to the Lord and
thus have the strength to withstand the temptation.[11] We can
never handle the temptation on our own, but we can have the
power necessary when we

admit our need of help and

turn to God for the lasting answer.

I confess my own struggle in times of difficulty and pain. I
have been tempted to bargain with God that

He might clearly reveal His power

He might renew my joy and strength

He might remove evil people from my path
He might overcome my thorns in the flesh
He might give new vitality to my work
so I might see that my labor expended was worth the effort. I
have been tempted to seek a response from God that would
assure me I was in His light, though I appeared to be in a
wilderness overshadowed by the clouds of evil about me. I
have not always received the answer in the way that I desired
it, but when at my best I have remembered that I have no
right to bargain with God—I have only to accept His love and
life freely offered me. And I know that when my heart is
stayed on Him, I can endure the wilderness, whatever form it
may assume! I have discovered

perfect peace in the midst of the wilderness experience
perfect peace in spite of the wilderness experience
perfect peace resulting from the wilderness experience!

The great English preacher, Leslie Weatherhead, wrote
about a rainy-day visit in Scotland. The skies were a dark
gray, and the hillsides looked dark and foreboding. Then, suddenly he could see a streak of light burst through, reminding
him that it was not night but day. Quickly the light would fade
away, and it would become gray and dark again. The occa-
sional rays of sunlight on that gloomy day reminded him that
above the clouds the sun was shining brightly. He did not
have to see the sunlight all the time to know that this was the
day God had created.[12] When we are willing to accept the fact
that God has not forsaken us, though He allows our day to be
overcast with the dark clouds of the world, we will be able to
resist the temptation to bargain with God to keep all the
clouds of the wilderness from us and give us only the bright-
ness and calm we desire. When we indeed trust the Lord as
our Rock we can learn to recognize Him, even when the loneliness and barrenness of life threaten to hide us from Him.

In the early 1980s a best-seller was Harold Kushner's
book, *When Bad Things Happen to Good People*. While he

has some good insights about suffering, I cannot agree with his conclusion that God "is not perfect" and that we must "forgive Him despite His limitations."[13] Kushner does help make the point that none of us is immune from problems, and neither should we point a finger of blame against ourselves or against God when we encounter severe obstacles. Ultimately, the real key is how we respond to our adversity.

The story is told of two Desert Fathers who lived in the same small area. The living arrangements required great humility and patience from both men. An observer wondered if the two were authentic in their fellowship and decided to test them. He went to visit these two, and after their time of greeting and prayer, the guest went outside and saw their little garden. With a stick he destroyed every plant he saw. Though they saw him, the two devout Christians did not say a thing to him, nor did they even show displeasure on their faces. After they had finished their evening prayers, they said to their guest,

"Sir, if you like, we can get one cabbage that is left, and cook it and eat it, for now it is time to eat."

When they had said this, this visitor fell on his knees and declared, "I give thanks to my God, for I see the Holy Spirit rests in you."[14]

In creating a difficult situation for the two devout men, the man had in actuality cast himself into a barren desert of envy and ill-will. The response the two holy men made to their own adversity was a model to the destructor about how he could find his way out of his spirit-threatening wilderness.

It seems that when life becomes entangled and problems are too large to handle that bargaining with God appears as a remedy. For those afraid of the wilderness

unsure about the wilderness

threatened by the wilderness

bargaining with God appears to be the "quick fix" and the escape hatch. Bargaining with God to take away pain

> to deal with our enemies
> to eliminate our problems
> to destroy our obstacles
> to elevate our work

gets us nowhere but indebted to the tempter! But when we
give our hearts and our lives afresh to our Living Lord who
loved us so much that He died for us, we can accept *His* bargain and receive His strength to go on in spite of

> our hurt
> our loneliness
> our pain and
> our lack of answers.

In the final scene of Archibald MacLeish's modern version
of Job called *J.B.*, J. B.'s wife tells him there is no justice in
life—only love. She concludes,

> The candles in churches are out,
> The stars have gone out in the sky.
> Blow on the coal of the heart
> And we'll see by and by. . . .[15]

Therein lies the power to resist temptation and have the hope
to endure suffering and pain

> "Blow on the coal of the heart
> And we'll see by and by. . . ."

In the wilderness experience wherein there is potential for
growth we need the warmth of the fires of the Spirit
to encourage

> to shed light
> > to revive
> > > to empower.

> Blow, Spirit, not to extinguish our fitful lights and distrusting
> fires

> Blow, Spirit, not to remove us from our wilderness experi-
> ences

Blow, Spirit, to kindle new light and warmth within us to
   sustain us in our time of temptation and difficulty
Blow, Spirit . . .
   Blow. . . .

On Distinguishing the Voices

Voices call out to us from every direction—political
economic
social
educational
racial
national
religious.

Voices call for our attention
our allegiance
our loyalty
our adherence
our faithfulness.

How do we determine which voices to heed?
How do we know which voices are authentic?
How do we decide which voices want our best?
How do we conclude which voices to follow?

4

On Distinguishing the Voices

One of the most fascinating stories of American folklore is *The Devil and Daniel Webster*. Stephen Vincent Benet wrote this compelling story a half century ago. With the story set in Webster's home state of New Hampshire, Benet wove a saga of Webster's greatness and his willingness to help the citizens in his New England State. Jabez Stone was a man in need of help. For years he had been a farmer whose success and good fortune were negative. He was not a bad man—but it seemed nothing ever worked out right for him!

If he planted corn, he got borers;
if he planted potatoes, he got blight.
He had good-enough land, but it didn't prosper him;
he had a decent wife and children,
   but the more children he had, the less there was to feed
   them.
If stone cropped up in his neighbor's field, boulders boiled up
in his. . . .[1]

It always seemed that Jabez Stone came up on the short end of the bargain. If he had a horse with an ailment, he would trade it for a horse with a worse aliment—and he would have to pay money besides the horse he traded!

One morning when two children had measles
              his wife was ill
          he broke his plow on a newly-discovered rock
      and his horse became sick

Jabez declared that his circumstances were enough to make a man want to sell his soul to the devil! And he declared he would do so for two cents! After making such a sweeping statement, he suddenly felt rather strange. He was a proud citizen of New Hampshire and a religious man, neither of whom bargained with the devil! The next evening a soft-spoken, well-dressed stranger rode up to Jabez Stone's house in a handsome buggy. Unwilling to break his word, Jabez was true to what he had said and he struck a bargain with the stranger who was the devil. And all at once his fortunes began to change! He became prosperous. His family was healthy. He was looked to as a community leader.

There was even talk of his running for the U.S. Senate. Once a year the devil checked on Jabez, and on the sixth year Jabez was reminded that their arrangement expired on the seventh. When he realized his life would surely be required of him, Stone argued earnestly and won only a three-year extension. And how quickly those last four years rolled by!

On the final day of the sinister bargain, Jabez visited Daniel Webster and asked for his help. Webster agreed and met the devil with Jabez that evening. But since the contract had been duly signed, there was no way for this great lawyer to get Jabez off. As a last resort, Webster requested a trial when the devil claimed to be an honest American citizen like everyone else. With Webster's consent, the devil summoned the judge and jury—all of whom were dead and currently living in hell! They were undoubtedly the meanest, most crooked, most vile thirteen who had ever lived in America! Well through the night Webster tried to plead with them, but with a glitter in their eyes they watched him. Suddenly Webster realized

. . . it was him they'd come for, not only Jabez Stone. He read it in the glitter of their eyes and in the way the stranger hid his mouth with one hand. And if he fought them with their own weapons, he'd fall into their power; he knew that, though he couldn't have told you how. It was his own anger and horror that burned in their eyes; and he'd have to wipe that out or the case was lost.[2]

He then began to appeal to the jury about what it meant
to be a man
  to be a free man
    to be an American.
He portrayed Jabez Stone as a typical American who had
faced hard luck and been trapped by the devil. When he finished, the jury decided to acquit Jabez and free him from the
devil's clutches. Webster knew he had beaten the devil, not
only for Jabez but for himself as well.

While Webster was holding the devil by the arm and collar,
Benet's folklore said the devil agreed with Daniel Webster
never again to bother Jabez Stone or any other people in New
Hampshire. When he had finished the agreement Webster
kicked the devil out of the house and out of New Hampshire!
Webster acted on the premise that once he had defeated the
devil, the satanic power over him was gone forever. We realize
that once we in Christ resist the devil, he cannot have ultimate
control over us, but the devil does continue to tempt us at
times opportune to him.

There are some important truths for us to grasp from this
folklore about the power of the devil. One is that in self-
piteous moments we can listen to the wrong voices and sell
our soul to the devil. Another is that none of us can fight the
devil on his own terms and win—we must respond from the
dignity of man as God created him; we must counter the devil
in the power and light God reveals to us. The story of man
across the ages is that we have repeatedly
  succumbed to the voice of the tempter and
  fallen to the plot of the evil one
thereby winding up in a bewildering wilderness of our own
choosing. Deuteronomy 6 is a descriptive reminder of man's
need to remember God's rule in life and to listen to His voice
and instruction. The writer said the Israelites were to be careful
not to forget that Yahweh God brought them out of the Egyptian slavery. Therefore they should stand in awe of Him
                    serve Him and
                    take His name seriously.

They were not to fall in with the customs of the people about them in Canaan and listen to the wrong voices that would lead them to false gods.

Just as those words were important in that day, even now we recognize how great is the temptation to experiment with the formulas our neighbors use for success and contentment. A person never wins success and happiness merely by copying the habits of his godless neighbors! The warning is spelled out in Deuteronomy 6:15. They were not to follow after the gods of the people about them—

for the Lord your God in the midst of you is a jealous God; lest the anger of the Lord your God be kindled against you, and he destroy you from off the face of the earth.

God arranged the covenant with Israel for the benefit of Israel, but that agreement required obedience to the will and direction of God's voice.

Just as people in Moses' day felt they could listen to the voice of the tempter in the wilderness and still come out in good shape, so people today think they can play with the power of sin and still be unscathed. But the facts are these:
- when we play with fire we do get burned, no matter how much we protest and claim we will not, and
- no people can turn their backs on God and escape His anger, wrath, and punishment!

That is not to indicate that one will immediately receive the due reward for his sin. If you appear to escape for a day
for a year
for a decade or
for a lifetime

God is still in control! You will be punished when you follow in the wilderness after Satan and false gods instead of humbling yourself before the One True God!

Perhaps now more than ever before in the history of our nation we are tempted to worship the tempter and follow false gods in business
in politics

      in education
        in family life
          in dating
            in friendships
               in neighborhoods and even
               in religion!

It is so easy for people in any day to think they are hearing the voice of God, when in fact they are adhering to the voice of Satan. The deceitful trick is that temptations to do evil approach us in a pleasant disguise in order to lure us into the demonic wilderness. It is reported that during the war between Great Britain and South Africa at the turn of this century, ammunition was transported in piano cases, and military messages were passed in the skins of melons![3] And so it is with the devil! He makes us think we are receiving pleasant music, when he sends the dischord of destructive relationships. He promises the sweet fruit of life, when in fact he feeds us the seeds of death! He offers us the ultimate freedom to "be ourselves" and "do our own thing," when in fact his chains are hidden behind the bright lights and dazzling sights! Surely now more than ever we need to discriminate between
what is true and false
  what is right and wrong
    what is good and evil
      what is godly and satanic
so we will no longer embrace the evil that will surely defeat and destroy both us and those about us!

    It may well be that when we have things going best for us or when we have the greatest potential that we wind up feeling empty and flat as we fall to the voice of the tempter. In his play, *Back to Methuselah,* George Bernard Shaw has Adam say to Eve:

    If only there may be an end some day, and yet no end! If only I can be relieved of the horror of having to endure myself forever! If only the care of this garden may pass on to some other gardener! If only the sentinel set by the Voice can be relieved! If only the rest and sleep that enable me to bear it

from day to day could grow after many days into an eternal
rest, an eternal sleep, then I could face my days, however
long they may last. Only there must be some end; some end.
I am not strong enough to bear eternity.[4]

Inevitably we will fall before the emptiness of life when we
lose the fine tuning that enables us to hear the amazing, abid-
ing voice of God! When we no longer care to hear the voice
of God, then everyday and everything are sheer horror and
unbearable stress.

It is important that we learn to distinguish the voices in our
wilderness experience. When we enter into the wilderness
experience voluntarily in order to be alone and deepen our
relationship with God, we may have the distraction of outside
  voices that will seek to tempt us away from the Spirit
  voices that will try to lure us out of God's will
voices that will attempt to distract us from obeying God.
When the wilderness experience is not of our own making, but
has come to us as a result of evil by others or circumstances
that have combined to create difficulty in our lives, we may
easily be diverted from trying to hear God's voice above the
maddening crowd of voices that promise easy solutions
            voices that offer instant success
        voices that assure constant pleasure.
We need to come to grips with the fact that temptation is
inescapable. Yet what we must determine is how we will respond to temptation the evil one places before us prior to the
time of temptation, so we can be prepared with our resources
and the power of God's Spirit when the tempter seeks to trap
us. When our son and daughter were learning to drive, one of
the training practices repeated over and over was "What . . .
if . . . ?"

What will you do if you run out of gas?
What will you do if the car goes into a left-sided skid?
What will you do if the car drops off the shoulder of the
    road?
What will you do if the "check engine" light comes on?

What will you do if someone tries to get into your car at a
   traffic light?

What will you do if your brakes fail?

What will you do if you have a blow out in a tire?

What will you do if someone runs a stop sign or traffic light
   when you have the right of way?

The point is, by facing the reality that emergencies do occur in
driving and seeking to know in advance how to respond to
that crisis, the driver has a much greater chance of surviving.

Similarly, by recognizing the reality of the tempter's voice
and determining in advance how to respond to his clever
ploys, we have a greater chance of resisting temptation's
wilderness and surviving in the power and presence of the
Lord. But rather than being prepared, it seems many have
come to the place where they feel: the position of ultimate
peace for humanity would be to have no struggle to do good
and no temptation to do evil. This attitude does nothing but
set us up as ready victims for the tempter! The fact is—
temptation is present in the world. And when we distinguish
the voice of God and follow Him through our wilderness experience, we can even grow stronger through our resistance to
temptation. God showed us in Jesus Christ all it means to be
human—

from birth to death

from joy to sorrow

from friendship to loneliness

from celebration to suffering

from acceptance to rejection

from life to death and

from death to life!

And as we examine the life and ministry of God's Son, we
find temptation in the midst of it! So why should we think we
would encounter anything less?

Matthew 4:8-10, mirrored in Luke 4:5-8, records one of
Jesus' wilderness temptations—the third one in Matthew and
the second one in Luke. One of the real advantages of study-

ing these temptations of Jesus is that we develop the awareness that part of being human is to be tempted! We need not feel guilty when we are tempted, nor should we feel we are not close to God when we are tempted. God knows about our temptations. Even Christ, the One who was without sin, was tempted. Indeed, the Scriptures give us clear evidence that

the closer we draw to God

the greater the effort we make to hear and heed Him

the more severe will our temptations be!

Jesus was first tempted to make food for Himself

then He was tempted to force God to act on His terms and

finally He was tempted to seize power for Himself—

power that not even the Father had given Him.

Satan claimed to have power over the world and thus the ability to give it to Jesus if only the Son of God would worship the tempter. But the fact is while the authority over the world belongs ultimately to God, He has permitted Satan in a limited sense to rule over an age that is passing away. Satan is alive and loose—and so long as people listen to his voice and follow him, he has a power over the forces of evil that pervade the world. The best students of this text tell us that Satan was tempting Jesus to use a shortcut to power and thereby fulfill the expectations of the Jewish people that Israel would be restored to the power of the Davidic Kingdom. To this end Judas Maccabaeus and the Zealots had worked.

Inevitably, to worship Satan is to adopt his methods

to select his weapons of power

to choose his tools of violence and

to rationalize destruction of others for one's

own end.[5]

Yet Satan is so subtle in how he speaks to us in order to wield his power over us when we fall to his temptation. The devil does not come to a religious person with a temptation to commit an overt act of evil. No, the devil is too smart to try, for he knows full well such a temptation would be resisted!

What the evil one does is to tempt us to do what is attractive
and pleasing to us rather than to do what we ought to do.
Our temptation comes in the form of leading us away from
what is best, even though we may do something that is good.
And the emotion the tempter plays on is that our following
him will give us power
    will give us authority
    will give us control
    will give us recognition.

   The temptation Satan offered Jesus at this point was an
appeal to His ambitions—
    not to engage in active evil
    but to accept the fact of evil
        to live with the presence of evil
        to come to terms with the power of evil
        to choose silence in the face of evil.[6]

It is important to recognize this distinction. When we listen to
the voice of Satan we may not be doing something that is considered illegal or even immoral by our peers, but we may be
selling our souls to the evil one all the same—succumbing to
the temptation to be less than what God is calling us to be in
Christ Jesus.

> There is no enacted law against hatred
> There is no easy way to measure prejudice
> There is no set scale to weigh spite
> There is no clear-cut standard for ambition
> There is no ready gauge to calculate gossip
> There is no established judgment for indifference
> There is no fixed criterion against the hunger for
>   power and control.

   Yet, these are sins that divert the believer's attention,
weaken his commitment to God, and harm his witness. Satan
works hard to convince believers to sell out and fall short
of what God intends them to be! You may be a constant bed
fellow with evil in others and yourself all the time you are con-

gratulating yourself for not being involved in the obvious evil of the world about you!

You may not be addicted to cocaine
   yet you may be addicted to having your own way!
You may not be addicted to heroin
   yet you may be addicted to caffeine!
You may not be addicted to shoplifting
   yet you may be addicted to withholding God's money!
You may not be addicted to child molesting
   yet you may be addicted to emotional battering!
You may not be addicted to attempting murder
   yet you may be addicted to destroying by hatred!
You may not be addicted to insider trading
   yet you may be addicted to subtle tax evasion!
You may not be addicted to alcohol
   yet you may be addicted to self-gratifying foods!
You may not be addicted to marital infidelity
   yet you may be addicted to ignoring your spouse!

So just when you think you are avoiding the obvious, known, public sins, you may be listening to the tempter's voice that is smothering you with sins that are literally controlling and consuming your spiritual life!

Carlyle Marney, the famed philosopher and conscience-prodder of many Christian pilgrims, was a good friend and helpful encourager during my years of ministry in North Carolina. He related an encounter he had with an aged professor he met while visiting in Lima, Peru. The professor had a burning interest in American, and in good English the teacher questioned Marney for some time about our land. When he turned to leave Marney he added, "Those of us who think most deeply here in Peru believe that our God has given peculiar blessings to your nation; we think she is a land of destiny and high calling. We only wish that her exports matched her calling."[7]

Marney wrote that as he looked about him at the cheap trinkets, gaudy jewelry, and pornographic literature, and as he was aware of the destructive American weapons being traded

and paraded around the world, he felt that professor's statement sear a hole in his conscience and memory. He sensed
not only that America's exports were not living up to her calling, but he also realized that the vast multitude of church
bodies and individual church members did not have output
from their lives that matched their high calling to discipleship
in Christ Jesus! And if we are not careful to distinguish the
voices, we will listen to the devil who tells us that what we do
or fail to do actually makes no difference. We face the grave
danger of trying to do something we think is important rather
than what God calls us to do, and in the long run we will lose
contact with His voice and consequently, meaning will evaporate from our lives. The wilderness experience requires keen
listening which can decipher the real from the fake

the true from the false

the lasting from the temporary

the godly from the evil

so that we will not be captured by the voice of the tempter.

Leo Tolstoy was clearly one of the greatest novelists who
ever lived. His *War and Peace* will always rank among the
monumental works of literature. His early life was spent in
sinful living, interestingly enough. He was not pleased with
how he was living, yet all his efforts to reform his life were
unsuccessful. He continued to be a victim of the voices he
sought to overcome. In describing the seductive voices that
drew him into sin, he wrote: "I knew where these voices came
from. I knew they were destroying my happiness; I struggled, I
lost. I fell asleep dreaming of fame and women . . . it was
stronger than I."[8]

As long as Tolstoy listened to the wrong voice, he failed to
have the strength to overcome his temptation and the sin he
was led to commit. His wilderness was of his own making,
constructed by weak resolve that succumbed to temptation.

Clearly there are two times when temptation troubles us
the most. One is when we are on the devil's ground and

the other is when we reach a new religious peak.

The frightening thing is that both an individual and a church can get on the devil's ground so easily and quickly! "History seems to show that powers of evil have won their greatest triumphs by capturing the organizations which were formed to defeat them," one person has concluded. He added, "When the devil has thus changed the contents of the bottles, he never alters the labels. The fort may have been captured by the enemy, but it still flies the flag of the defenders."[9]

Do you grasp the subtlety of falling to the temptation the writer described? Satan seeks to overtake both religious works as well as Christian churches.

He does not change the label.

He does not change the flag.

He does not change the name.

He does not change the programs.

He does not change the promotion.

But he does change the insides of persons and churches when they are given over to him!

Those who live on his ground feel somehow immune to the consequences of their listening to the wrong voices and heeding one other rather than Christ.

The story is told about a chauffeur who drove a car exceeding 70 MPH out of Trenton, New Jersey. A highway patrolman chased him and finally waved him over to the roadside. When asked if he knew he was driving faster than 70 MPH, the driver smiled and said that was OK with him. When the state trooper warned he would give him a ticket, the man replied that it was fine—he could give him two or three! The frustrated officer told the speedster that he could be fined and also put in jail! The driver said that was OK with him! The patrolman blurted out and asked just who this man was. He smiled and replied he was the driver for the warden of the State Penitentiary and that he was already serving a life sentence![10] There are times we feel so comfortable on the devil's turf that we easily fall for his temptation and listen to his voice as though the consequences make no difference!

We also face the temptation of heeding the wrong voice

when we reach a new religious peak. There are no people more excited or more vulnerable than those who feel they have attained a new religious high! After forty days Jesus spent alone with the Father in the wilderness, Satan spiritually and emotionally assaulted Him with three temptations. Some people would never open themselves to such an experience of solitude, meditation, silence, and retreat in the first place. Many of those who come away from some spiritual and emotional high are often guilty of immediately failing to listen to the right voice. Jesus did not fall to Satan's temptation. He quoted almost verbatim Deuteronomy 6:13 as He rebuffed the devil and refused to worship him, saying, "You shall worship the Lord your God and him only shall you serve."

The wilderness experience had strengthened, enriched, and directed Jesus, and He was therefore able to withstand Satan's powerful attacks. It was *true* worship that formed the boundaries of Jesus' life, and from that authentic worship His obedience and spiritual power flowed. All temptations are toward the worship of false gods.

The temptation of theft bows to the god of money

The temptation of immorality bows to the god of lust

The temptation of hedonism bows to the god of pleasure

The temptation of hatred bows to the god of pride

The temptation of havoc bows to the god of boredom

The temptation of prejudice bows to the god of ego.

Therefore, when Jesus made His response to Satan's voice after listening to the voice of His Father, Jesus literally told Satan to go away and leave Him alone

to go to hell where he belonged!

And the Gospels tell us that Satan did leave Him! However, Luke adds the word of reality at the conclusion of verse 13, ". . . [Satan] departed from Him until an opportune time."

All of Jesus' temptations were not ended when He resisted those three, for He was tempted in every manner like as we are, yet without sin, Hebrew 4:15 instructs us.

So many church members never reach the point where

they listen carefully enough to God to defeat the tempter. There is an amazingly powerful quality about a person who has overcome the powers of evil. When, with the unseen strength of the Holy Spirit, we go one-on-one against Satan and defeat him, then we are able to hear God more clearly and conquer other wiles of the devil more effectively and efficiently than ever before. There are some experiences, similar to the conclusion of Jesus' stay in the wilderness, which, when we have completed them, cause us to know that life can no longer trip us, and no one can any longer coerce us away from God!

A newcomer once asked an established worker why he was always happy and seemed to be upset by nothing. The man replied that nothing bothered him after he had injured his hand. He held up a scarred hand that had been badly damaged and then told about the time several years earlier when he had been sick for almost a year, had lost his job, and did not know how he could support his family. He was called for an interview for a new job, wrecked his car on the way, and lost part of his hand in the wreck! But after he recovered from the wreck he landed a job. Now he knew that nothing could overwhelm him since he made it through that experience. Now he could laugh at anything.[11]

Through a careful discernment of the spiritual voices calling to Him and the strength of His victory over temptation and sin, Jesus exercised an amazing power to develop spiritual strength through His wilderness experience. We may still have a hard, tedious time distinguishing the voices so we may hear God's voice above all the noise and din of the world, but when we pay that price, we can rest assured that we belong to God, and the devil cannot possess or control us. In God's power and by listening to His voice we can endure any wilderness!

You may be wondering how you can learn to so listen to God that you will have the power you need in the wilderness. There is no pat answer or easy shortcut for you, but our Lord promises He will help you through the power of His Spirit. An author wrote of a summer day when he was walking in a remote area and found a three-year-old boy rubbing his eyes and crying softly. He asked him who he was and where he lived, but all he heard in reply was the name Tony. The man picked Tony up in his arms and saw the boy's feet bruised and bleeding from walking barefoot on rocky roads. After a while the writer asked the little boy, "Tony, how are we going to find your home?" With fresh confidence and amazing courage, Tony looked at the man and declared, "You just start walking and I'll tell you when we get there!"[12]

Like Tony, we who walk and live in a wilderness need to be still and listen to our Rescuer's voice! Then we can climb into the Holy Arms of the Father who will enable us to travel the remotest regions of life's dark landscape and take us safely home! He will bind up our bruised and bleeding spirits and give us wilderness vision and
                wilderness hearing!

We need only listen intently to God's voice as we travel through life, knowing He will tell us when we are where He wants us to be. Our problems may be immense and our patience worn thin, but we need not fall to temptation and sell our birthright to obtain what we need. Distinguish God's voice, heed Him, and defeat the devil. Go on through the wilderness. Go on!

Spiritual Support System

God says He will take care of His Children.
Do you believe that?

God says He knows us by name
    He knows our rising up and going to sleep
   He knows the number of hairs on our head.
Do you believe that?

God says He will never abandon or forsake us.
Do you believe that?

We are a people who are
   frayed   tense   distrustful
        disturbed   troubled
  worried   upset   anxious.

Who will answer our yearning hearts?
  Who will minister to our hurting spirits?
    Who will direct our weary steps?
     Who?
       Immanuel
       El-Shaddai
       Dayspring!

5

Spiritual Support System

A half century ago a traveler was driving across the farm-lands of the Midwest. Upon noticing a strange mound out in a field, he stopped at the nearby farmhouse to ask about it. The farmer walked with the stranger over to the mound, demonstrating no obvious interest whatsoever. The excited traveler exclaimed, "My dear sir, I may be mistaken, but I believe this is a relic of the Mound Builders. Have you ever thought of excavating to find out for yourself what is under this pile of earth?"

The middle-aged farmer very quickly answered the question, "This farm has been in our family for four generations. My grandfather never dug in that mound, neither did his father, and my father never explored it, and you can bet your last dollar I'll never dig it up."[1]

What a classic example of a man who was so bound by traditional practice
   traditional thought
      traditional habit
         traditional belief
that he was not open to a new experience, no matter how exciting and transforming it might have been! And surely that closed-minded, tradition-bound farmer is a reflection of the multitudes of people in every generation who stand on the edge of an amazing discovery of God's love and grace, only to walk away in ignorance because the information did not com-

pute in their minds or the possibility did not fit into their tradition!

A notable exception is found in Daniel 3 when King Nebuchadnezzar's countrymen were jealous of the positions held by faithful Jewish exiles. The Chaldeans determined to get rid of three who held positions of influence they desired for themselves. After the pagan king had ordered that everyone was to worship the golden image he had established, Shadrach, Meshach, and Abednego continued to bow down and worship only Yahweh God. When their envious competitors had them watched, caught, and brought before the king, the three devout worshipers of Yahweh declared they would not worship or serve any false god. Their declaration angered the king, and he ordered that the furnace was to be heated seven times the normal temperature, and the three of them were to be cast into it for their punishment. The fire was so hot that the soldiers who placed them in it were consumed by the heat and died!

The angry king went to see that the job was done properly, and he questioned if they had not put only three men into the fire. When told that was the number, he anxiously observed, "But I see four men loose, walking in the midst of the fire, and they are not hurt; and the appearance of the fourth is like a son of the gods."[2]

Nebuchadnezzar then called for the three faithful Israelites to be removed from the furnace. He announced, "Blessed be the God of Shadrach, Meshach, and Abednego, who has sent his angel and delivered his servants, who trusted in him. . . ."[3]

Because of their faithfulness to Yahweh God the king declared that no one was to speak or do anything against their God without being punished by death. And then he promoted the three young men to even more responsible positions!

Unlike the farmer who saw the same mound in his field which three generations of his family had observed without doing anything, King Nebuchadnezzar observed and admitted the unusual nature of what transpired and therefore changed his mind and actions.

He admitted the strength of the Israelite's God.

He declared their God had sent an angel to rescue them.

He altered his view about worshiping their God and gave
  them complete protection.

The king recognized that the three faithful Hebrews had a
spiritual support system that sustained them, and he would
not allow anyone to deny them their faith or to tamper with
their religious practices. His witness of the God who delivered
them by one "like a son of the gods" in the fiery furnace
caused Nebuchadnezzar to change his approach with the
three men.

Across the centuries there have not been many as courageous or able as Nebuchadnezzar to recognize their error or
to alter their view. The course most have taken about any
matter—and especially religion—is to cling to what they have
always held to be true and ignore any other view presented.
John Denver sings a ballad of a man

who loved the sun

  who talked to animals

    who said animals talked to him

      who would not overlook a single tree for the whole
        forest.

Because he was different and viewed nature in a manner unlike those about him, he was driven out of the community and
called insane. After the ballad describes the pathos of this
man's treatment by his fellows, the singer then questions that
perhaps the man was right. Why should they disbelieve what
he said simply because they had never heard the animals? But
such a question is usually quickly squelched, for it is easier to
maintain our traditional view when we ignore any and all vari-
ations to what we have thought and believed in the past.

The final verse in the paragraph of Matthew's account
of Jesus' temptations in the wilderness reads:

"Then the devil left him, and behold, angels came and ministered to him."[4]

Because the concept of angels is not a common one in
our modern experience we tend to pass over this statement as

naïve and unimportant, or else we totally miss its meaning. I do not mean to point an accusing finger at the reader without confessing that I had written and spoken for twenty-five years before I ever dealt specifically with angels and their ministry! It was a dramatic time for me when this declaration about angels leaped from the page of my Bible into my heart and mind.

Definitions and descriptions of angels in the Bible reveal that the word *angel* translates the Hebrew and Greek words which means "messenger" or "one sent."

The principle responsibility of angels was to communicate directives of God usually spoken in the form of an urgent command. The second major task of angels was to protect the faithful ones of God, either individually or collectively.[5] Angels are invisible spirits who may appear to mankind in human form. They were created by God above man. Angels are not God and thus are not all-powerful or cannot be all places at once—but angels do have an important role in God's dealing with man, a role which most of us by tradition have not taken seriously . . .

Interestingly enough, since the Middle-Ages belief in angels has been on a downswing. And with greater intellectual discoveries and scientific achievements during this century, by the 1960s it was predicted that all belief in the supernatural would cease by the 1970s! But do you realize just what has taken place? During the last decade we have not witnessed the termination of belief in the supernatural. On the contrary, we have seen a rapid *increase* of belief in the supernatural—but much of it has been *negative!* We have seen stacked on top of one another

ouija boards	astrology along with
white magic	demon worship and
seances	Satan worship!

During the 1980s we have been flooded with books
movies
stories and
testimonials

of demon possession and Satan worship. Yet this observation
is but a backdrop to affirm there is much more in the Bible
about angels than Satan and demons! As a matter of fact,
there are more than three hundred references to angels in the
Bible! While scholars and skeptics have bled the power and
strength from the belief in angels by saying that other ancient
peoples and religions had their angelic bodies—and therefore
we need not believe in them—now more than ever before we
need to understand what the Bible means when it declares
". . . angels came and ministered to him."

Now we may not ever know all about angels, but should
that keep us from realizing and experiencing the spiritual support system they offer? As a parallel question, we might ask
ourselves if we understand how geese know how to migrate
thousands of miles or how swallows know how to return to
their home each year or how salmon know how to swim up-
stream to spawn their young? We cannot fully comprehend
the seemingly supernatural capacity of these creatures God
created, but our lack of understanding does not prevent our
knowing about them and marveling at what they achieve.
Therefore, when we come to read the final statement about
Jesus' temptations, we do not have to know everything about
angels to realize that Jesus received their ministry! The Greek
word translated "ministered" in Matthew 4:11 is related to the
word we read elsewhere in the New Testament and translates
as "deacon." Just as deacons were conceived of to meet the
needs of the church members, so the angels came to meet the
needs of Jesus. It is interesting to note that we do not know
how the angels ministered

how many angels there were
in what form they appeared
how long they stayed with Christ
or exactly what they did.

We trust they were visible to Christ and cared for His physical needs and restored His spiritual strength. Yet, the truth is:
it really does not matter so much what the angels did, and

how they did it, as it matters that they did minister to Him as
the Scripture records! Those whom the Heavenly Father created and whom the human eye does not normally behold
came and cared for our weary Lord after forty days of wilderness fasting and three exhausting temptations!

Such thought and reflection on the biblical teaching of
angels can only make us wonder how often we may have
been ministered to by an angel unawares or how often we
have seen but did not recognize an angel. In Santa Fe, New
Mexico, there is an old Spanish chapel called Loretto Chapel.
At the rear of the chapel is a choir loft. For some unknown
reason the builders omitted a stairway to the choir loft, making
it necessary to use a step ladder to climb the twenty-two feet
up into the loft. The priests were fearful that men and women
alike would fall and injure themselves on the treacherous ladder. Then one day an unknown carpenter appeared and built
an architectural masterpiece! He constructed a circular stair-
case twenty-two feet high without any central support. It
makes two complete 360-degree turns with its thirty-three
steps. He used no nails—just wooden pegs—in his construction. He departed as quietly as he came. No one in the terri-
tory had ever heard of such a carpenter, nor did they ever see
or hear of him afterwards! The people at Loretto Chapel concluded he was one of God's angels!

The Bible reveals interesting truths about the work and
ministry of angels. Maybe more importantly, the Bible underscores that angels are available to us, but we ignore them! First
Kings 19 records the wilderness experience of Elijah who fled
the wicked Queen Jezebel right after his stunning victory over
the priests of Baal. In his anxious weariness in the wilderness
Elijah wished that he might die, and then an angel came to
him with food and water. After he ate and slept, the angel
came to him the second time with food and drink, so Elijah
would have strength for the long journey to Sinai.

Acts 12 records the account of Peter's imprisonment after
Herod had killed James. Herod was supposedly going to kill

Peter also. During the night an angel came to him when he was chained between two guards in prison. His chains fell loose, and, following the angel's directions, Peter dressed and escaped with the angel from the prison. Peter admitted that at first he did not know if he were dreaming or if he truly were being freed. When he got out of prison the angel left him and Peter concluded, "Now I am sure that the Lord has sent his angel and rescued me from the hand of Herod and from all that the Jewish people were expecting."[6]

The writer of Hebrews directs us, "Do not neglect to show hospitality to strangers, for thereby some have entertained angels unawares."[7]

The Bible does not raise a question about the validity of angels. The Bible is full of references to angels and calls us to trust its faithful witness of God's provision for the believer's spiritual support system.

When Billy Graham wrote his book, *Angels: God's Secret Agents,* he admitted that most Christians today fail to defeat their spiritual enemies because they do not rely on God's help available through His angels. Graham wrote: ". . . the closer I get to the frontiers of the Christian faith the more faith in angels I find among believers. . . . God is using His angels as ministering spirits."[8]

Billy's wife, Ruth, was the daughter of missionaries to China. Her father told of an incident which occurred in 1942. After the Japanese had defeated the Chinese, a Japanese army truck drove up in front of a Christian book store. The timid shopkeeper realized they had come to take away his stock of Christian books and materials. The soldiers jumped off the truck and started for the door, but before they reached it, a Chinese gentleman stepped through the door in front of them. The shopkeeper who knew everyone in the town had never seen the man before.

And strangely, while he was with the storekeeper, it seemed as though the soldiers could not come in. They stood around outside the store, waiting and looking in. For two

hours they waited outside. Inside, the gentleman asked what
the trouble was. When told about the possible confiscation
and destruction of Christian literature, the Chinese gentleman
prayed with the shopkeeper and gave encouragement for two
hours. Finally, the soldiers climbed back into their truck and
drove away. Then the gentleman left the store without buying
or asking about any merchandise. Could that stranger have
been an angel? When the shopkeeper told the owner, who
also knew everyone in the city but did not know the stranger,
they both concluded it was an angel sent from God to save
the store and its supplies![9]

Psalm 91 speaks magnificently of the watchcare God provides through His angels in the wilderness experience of life.
The psalmist describes
    the shelter
    the refuge
    the cover
    the defense
that will protect the believer from the terror of night and the
destruction of the day.
"For he will give his angels charge of you to guard you in all
    your ways."[10]
While Satan turned around and quoted verses 11-12 in his
earlier temptation of Jesus, we hear these words as sheer
comfort that God does care about us and through the protection of His angels we can live without fear! We can look evil in
the face with a smile, knowing that God is with us to give us
    strength
    power
    guidance
    deliverance and
    hope!
We tend to overlook two facets of the spiritual support
system God offers us. We have ignored the presence and protection of angels which benefit us mightily, and we have over-
looked the means we have of overcoming the devil. While the

tempter seeks to lure us to rationalize and disobey God in order to please ourselves, we need to ready our defense against him. The New Testament is filled with direction for us.

"Be on guard, lest Satan get an advantage."[11]

"Give no opportunity to the devil."[12]

"Be sober and vigilant."[13]

"Resist the devil and he will flee from you."[14]

Do you realize what the Scripture is saying to us? There is a spiritual warfare under way in this world, and we have the means and support available to us to defeat the evil one if we are prepared and call upon and respond to God's provision! The angels are aware of our condition and spiritual need, as Luke 15:10 testifies, ". . . there is joy before the angels of God over one sinner who repents."

Perhaps one of the most impressive accounts of God's support system for those who are His own is found in 2 Kings 6. The King of Syria was upset in his continued losses to Israel and asked how he was being defeated. His spies told him that the prophet Elisha was the cause—he kept the Israelite king informed of what the Syrian army was going to do. So the angry Syrian king set out for Elisha. They came at night to Dothan where Elisha was. The next morning Elisha's servant looked out and clasped his hands in utter dismay, asking, "Alas, my master! What shall we do?"

And God's man replied, "Fear not, for those who are with us are more than those who are with them."[15]

Then Elisha prayed that God would open his servant's eyes. And God did, and the servant beheld what was present—a whole host of angels who commanded chariots to help and defend Elisha. Do we today go around clasping our hands crying out,

"Alas . . . what shall we do?"

because we do not believe that

"*those* who are *with us* are *more*
than *those* who are *with them*"?

Do we have no confidence in God's provision that His angels

will minister to us, even as they did to His Son, our Lord? Do we falter in our wilderness and grow weaker rather than rely on the powerful support system God has created for His own? Do we fearfully stumble around in the barren, remote regions without the confidence and security God affords us through His holy angels?

One night bandits surrounded a mission compound in which there were several hundred women and children refugees who were new believers. The resilient missionary was ill with malaria and was concerned about how these new believers would react when the bandits came and looted the mission compound. The missionary prayed more earnestly than ever that God would deliver them so they would not lose faith in the protection she had told them God would provide. The missionary arose from her sick bed and comforted the anxious refugees while the bandits were raiding buildings all around the mission compound. They left before dawn without ever touching the mission area! When the looters had departed, neighbors came from three sides of the compound, all asking the same question,

"Who were those four people, three sitting and one standing, quietly watching from the top of your house all night long?"

The missionary told them she had no one on her house. But when the neighbors insisted they had seen the four, the missionary quietly concluded that God had sent His angels to guard His children in their time of need![16]

The old spiritual stressed the truth in these words:

> All night, all day,
> Angels watching over me, My Lord;
> All night, all day,
> Angels watching over me!

You may be skeptical in this reminder of the spiritual support system the Bible says God provides His own. God has made provision for His children!

He will never leave or forsake us!

He will send His angels to minister to us even as He did
His only Son!
We may not see or recognize the angels, but they will be with
us to give us support! So fear not! Do not disbelieve because
of lack of experience. Walk on through the very teeth of evil,
for God is with you! You will not be overcome. Your wilderness journey is patrolled by God's angels!

Behind the Facade of Praise

We feel the excitement of applause.
We sense the awesomeness of the adoration.
We remember joyful feelings about great festivals.
We seldom think about the meaning behind the festive cele-
    brations as we journey through the wilderness.

We offer ready praise in spite of emptiness
                    praise in the midst of confusion
                    praise because of habit
                    praise out of expectation
yet rarely do we examine the motives of our hearts.

We need to learn to lay aside our masks
                    cast off our facades
                    relinquish our pretense
                    remove our veneer
                    eliminate our hypocrisy and
                    encounter God through praise in the wilderness.

The King of kings and Lord of lords awaits our praise.
We cannot truly give it until we have replaced the empty fa-
    cade of praise with genuine commitment.

6

Behind the Facade of Praise

Nearly four centuries ago the English literary genius, William Shakespeare, wrote the play *Julius Caesar*. Caesar had been a leader and general in the first century BC in a government that was only nominally democratic. When his foes became jealous of his power and influence, they sought to have his army disbanded. Caesar refused and crossed the Rubicon River as a sign he was going to seize absolute control of the Roman Empire. It took him four years to do so, but he returned to Rome as the master of the Empire. He proved to be a man who cared for and gave generously to the needs of the common people. He was loved and respected by the multitudes in the Roman Empire, but a group of wealthy, influential men plotted to murder him.

A close "friend" of Caesar was Brutus, a man who was in the thick of the plot to overthrow Caesar. When the half-dozen men pulled their daggers to stab Caesar to death, he tried to dodge their weapons and escape his murder. But then he looked up and saw Brutus's dagger raised and ready to plunge into his body, and he covered his face and submitted to his death with the painful line:

"Et tu, Brute! [And you, too, Brutus!] Then fall, Caesar!"[1] His betrayal by a trusted friend was more than Caesar could bear. He was so overwhelmed by this act of decep-

tion and desertion that he made no more attempt to save
himself.

Shakespeare masterfully revealed how naïve the people
were and how easily they were manipulated by those who
spoke to them. When Brutus declared in public that he
loved Caesar

but loved Rome more and thus killed him to free the
Empire from an ambitious man

he was applauded! They even cried out that a statue should
be erected of Brutus, and he should become Caesar! Clearly,
Shakespeare pointed out the hopelessness of wiping out tyr-
anny as long as people are willing

to be controlled by another and
to be dictated to by another.

Their offer to make Brutus their ruler demonstrated the
contradiction of their approval of his murdering Caesar in order to free them from an absolute ruler! When people give up
their power to think and decide for themselves, they will
always slide from one dictator to another

from one manipulator to another
from one power source to another
from one master to another.

Anthony, another supporter of Caesar and an ambitious
man in his own right, swayed the people in opposition
to Brutus and his assassins when he made a moving
speech. Shakespeare gave Anthony some of his most
famous lines

The evil that men do lives after them;
The good is often interred with their bones. . . .[2]

Anthony then proceeded to describe the knife of the traitor,
Brutus, whom Caesar so dearly loved.

This was the most unkindest cut of all;
For when the noble Caesar saw him stab,
Ingratitude, more strong than traitor's arms,

> Quite vanquished him; then burst his mighty heart;
> And . . . great Caesar fell.[3]

By the time that Anthony had read Caesar's will to the people, telling them he gave to every Roman citizen a substantial sum of money, the people formed a mob and ran Brutus and his conspirators out of Rome! Before the play ends Brutus and his main colleague, Cassius, had killed themselves after failing to gain control of the Roman Empire. Anthony said of Brutus that of all the conspirators only he acted out of a desire to help others, and even he used the wrong means to accomplish his end. The man who betrayed a friendship with Caesar for what he thought was a better deal wound up with failure, guilt, and no desire to live.

We all have read and many have experienced the reality of the emptiness of praise from those who say the right words in the right places, and yet all the while work to destroy a person. What makes the pain so much deeper is when one who appears to be a friend
is in fact a destructive enemy.
We expect evil from the hands of those who are openly opposed, but it is more painful to be cut down by those who claim and appear to be supportive friends.

What a heavy burden it is to realize Jesus experienced rejection
opposition
undercurrent
antagonism
attacks
on every hand! He was countered and betrayed
by His neighbors
by His close friends
by the religious leaders and
by the masses!
His first resistance came not long after He left the desert

wilderness to experience the spiritual wilderness among hostile, indifferent, complacent religious people.

Mark 6 reminds us that when Jesus went to Nazareth to teach and preach in the synagogue, the people were astonished at His wisdom (v. 2). However, instead of of adhering to their praise of His ability, they began to complain

they began to take offense
and they began to reject Him!

And Jesus said:

"A prophet is not without honor, except in his own country, and among his own kin, and in his own house." And he could do no mighty work there, except that he laid his hands upon a few sick people and healed them. And he marveled because of their unbelief.[4]

Thus, early in His ministry Jesus felt the sting of rejection behind the facade of the praise offered for His wisdom, mercy, power, and healing. This was the pattern throughout three years of ministering to people enshrouded in their self-made wilderness—

rejection and betrayal veiled in
pretentious interest and praise.

His close friends and followers claimed to love and support Him. They praised His deeds and pledged their loyalty.

Yet it became quite evident they were working for themselves, and not for Christ! It was not only Judas who betrayed Christ. In Mark 10 we see that James and John asked for the two most powerful positions in Jesus' kingdom.[5] Luke reminds us that while sitting at the table for their Last Meal together the disciples broke out into an argument about which of them should be thought of as the greatest.[6] Plainly, Jesus had felt what it was like to hear praise heaped upon Him when praise had no roots or meaning. His friends had said the right things at the right times, but they were only looking out for their selfish interests.

How well Jesus understood the agony of the psalmist. The psalmist confessed he could bear being taunted and oppressed by a stated enemy or avowed adversary, but his deep pain came in the realization that he was being undercut by one who pretended to be his friend.

> We used to hold sweet converse together;
> within God's house we walked in fellowship.[7]

The psalmist knew there could be no greater hurt than that inflicted by one who claimed to be a spiritual kinsman. He described the betrayer whose mask of praise finally slipped off—

> His speech was smoother than butter,
> yet war was in his heart;
> his words were softer than oil,
> yet they were drawn swords.[8]

Jesus knew the devastation of smooth, soft words while underneath there were butchering daggers! How surprising it must have been, then, even as it is now, when it became obvious that those who appeared to be supporters were in fact opponents! The point is, very few people ever look beneath the surface. In any circle—including even a place of worship— there are all the appearances of peace
of calm
of pleasantness
of love
of support
of agreement
when beneath the surface there may lie unchained hatred and unleashed spite!
Those who view only the smiles and clichés may miss the destructive work going on behind the scenes. Jesus knew! And He suffered because of the facade of praise.

A painting entitled "The Shadow of Death" portrays Jesus working in the Nazareth carpentry shop. He is conclud-

ing His work at the end of the day, and the sun's last rays
are entering the room through the open door. The young
man who is completing His labor at the bench raises up
for a moment to stretch His cramped arms. At that moment
the setting sun catches His figure and casts His shadow
on the back wall of the carpenter shop, forming a cross!
The artist thus communicates that from the beginning of
Jesus' ministry, He was living in a wilderness experience
with death looming over Him![9] From the first miracle at
the wedding feast and His first teaching and preaching
Jesus heard the verbal praise heaped over the top of the
nonverbal judgmental condemnation. And the shadow
of the facade grew larger and larger with each passing day!
Each word of praise was accompanied by an increasing
feeling of
    unbelieving jealousy on the one hand and
    self-serving non-commitment on the other.
It appeared to be only a matter of time before the empty
praise became zealous destruction!

    Throughout His ministry Jesus had heard the insincere
words of the religious hierarchy of His day. Their thin facade
wore out rather quickly. After all,
    if Jesus were right
    then they were wrong!
If Jesus won the people to His side, the hierarchy's prestige
and influence would evaporate. Besides, their very way of life
was threatened! Jewish historian Josephus stated that 20,000
priests ministered in the Temple! Some would work only one
week out of the year and yet draw a full year's salary. On top
of the Roman taxes were added the Temple taxes for this
inefficient
    listless
      dying
        uninspiring
          traditional

noncompassionate
self-serving

practice of religion! In order to maintain their control and guarantee their income, the priests had country estates where animals were grown for Temple sacrifice. When the priests rejected the other animals brought to the Temple, their own were sold! No one else was allowed to sell, and they set the rate of exchange for the Jewish people who came to the Holy City from around the world. They oppressed the people, and Jesus dared turn His search-light on their evil deeds overflowing from behind their disguises of religiosity. If Jesus succeeded, the religious hierarchy knew they would be doomed. And they could not tolerate that possibility.

The religious leaders of the first century did what every scheming individual or group has done from that day to this! They worked hard behind the scenes to pull the wool over the people's eyes. They made the Savior look like a scoundrel so their sandalous deeds would appear helpful. They were so effective in launching their facade that the people did not realize they were being duped. And by the time they saw what the real truth was, they were too embarrassed to change their course!

The manipulated persons of the first century were like those manipulated in Germany of the 1930s. In the years leading up to Hitler's launching of World War II, an unknown house painter began making speeches to the umemployed working classes. Before many months passed, the masses endorsed him as their Füerher, and he convinced the estab-lished church of Germany that he was following the right course. When many of the German people finally woke up to Hitler's murderous plot to control the world and destroy all unlike himself, they were too embarrassed to admit their mis-take and take corrective action. The same thing happened during the 1950s in Cuba when Castro led a revolution. At first the leadership convinced the people that he was the savior of the nation. By the time the people realized he was fast becoming a dictator, they were so hesitant and embarrassed at what they had done for and with Castro that they did little within the country to oppose him. How many times a nation

a company

an organization

a group

has been overtaken and destroyed before the people realized what was happening. Even more unnerving is to realize how a few people can sway a mass when they are clever in their approach and words. A facade of praise in an evil wilderness maze can often work wonders for those who are masters of manipulation.

The religious leaders of Jesus' day saw Him as competition for their corrupt practices. Since they wanted things left as they had always been before

they sought to discredit Him with the people

they attempted to undercut His effectiveness

they questioned His ability and authority

they chose to try to run Him out of town

they decided to have Him put to death!

Because they did not want their system tampered with, they had to get rid of the One whose life unmasked the darkness of their evil spilling out over their facade of praise!

Ultimately the masses of the people who shouted their praise cried out for the destruction of Jesus. The people were enticed initially by their self-centered interest and fell in love with His preaching, were thrilled at His miracles, believed once again in their nation and affirmed His Messiahship with their own definition of the messianic mission—And how fickle those people were! They wanted bread

privilege

wealth and

power

and were willing to give Jesus empty praise and follow Him as long as it seemed He would provide their wishes!

How hollow was their praise! They did not mean what they said! They only wanted Jesus on their side so they could get from Him what they desired! They were fickle

> they were self-serving
> and they were uncom-
> mitted!

Maybe they showed up at the right places and appeared to possess the right enthusiasm, but they did not move beyond wanting what they wanted when they wanted it for themselves. They expected "swords flashing

> banners flying
> revolt against Rome
> Jewry reinstated in power.
> A voice cannot be popular with the
> crowd when it stabs at men's moral
> iniquities and dismisses as irrelevant
> their popular hopes."[10]

The people sloughed off their praise on Palm Sunday because it meant nothing more than a mob reaction on a pleasant spring day! They had all the signs before them which they refused to read because they remained in their chosen wildernesses and were concerned only about what they wanted and hoped for. Because of their inconsistency and disappointment for His lack of performance, they changed their minds about Him and determined that He had to be stopped.

Zechariah prophesied about the Prince of Peace who would come riding triumphantly into Jerusalem on a colt. This was a sign of the long-awaited King, the promised Messiah. At the outset of Jesus' final entry into Jerusalem it appeared that He was being recognized and received as the King He was. The poet observed,

Yet the days were becoming ever more ominous, more
grim.
There was no stirring the hearts of men through love;
Their eyebrows knit in disdain.
And now, the epilogue. Finis. . . .
Then the dark forces of the Temple
Gave Him up to be judged by the offscourings.
And, with the same fervor with which they once sang His
praises,
Men now reviled Him.[11]

While whispers and rumors flooded the city, Jesus remembered what had taken place throughout His life and ministry.
While the mumblings
            grumblings and
            plottings
grew thicker and louder, Jesus kept His eyes on
    the needs of the multitudes and
        the cares of the individuals.
The Gospels tell us that His life was filled with compassion
for people "because they were like sheep without a shep-
herd."[12] Jesus wept over Jerusalem following His grand entry
on Palm Sunday. Matthew recorded His declaration about the
people of that city,

O Jerusalem, Jerusalem, killing the prophets and stoning
those who are sent to you! How often would I have gathered
your children together as a hen gathers her brood under her
wings, and you would not! Behold your house is forsake
and desolate. For I tell you, you will not see me again, until
you say, "Blessed is he who comes in the name of the
Lord."[13]

Jesus realized the people were choosing to remain blinded
in the wilderness rather than to follow His voice to His
Father!
        Do you sense the compassion of Christ?
            Yet we remember the pain of His rejection!

Do you feel the great love of Christ?
Yet we hear the pretense of the praise offered Him!
Do you sense the grace and power of Christ?
Yet we recall His willing suffering for our salvation!
He was never untrustworthy
                    self-serving or
                        uncommitted.

He heard the directive of His Heavenly Father, and He refused to hide behind any facade! He faced squarely what God called Him to be and do, and thus He rejected repeatedly Satan's temptation to live for him. While the great majority of people across the ages, including even now, abdicate their thinking privileges and listen to someone who claims to have all the answers, Jesus continued to listen to and obey His Father and not Satan. He took great risks, even that of being trapped and His life required, so that He might offer endless light
  everlasting love and
    eternal life!

He chose the lonely wilderness because only there could He hear distinctly the Father's direction. He preached the wilderness experience of the narrow road that few travel, the small gate that few enter.

Yet He received only empty praise for what He did. And
    that was what those people rejected and
    that is what people today are rejecting!

A half-century ago the novelist wrote of the migrant farm workers in California who were seeking to overcome the suppression of the land owners. Two men led almost a thousand workers in a nearly successful movement for rights and fairness. The movement was cut short when, under the guise of an emergency, the two leaders were called out into the darkness to help a friend. Rather than helping a hurting friend, they were ambushed and one of the leaders was killed instantly. The novelist does not clearly state who did the

murdering—the land owners or the strikers who turned
against the leader.

In one sense it made little difference, for the facade of
praise and support had set in on the migrants whom the
leader was attempting to help. He could not stand against his
opponents on both sides who wanted him out of the way. In a
sense both those he opposed and those he helped murdered
him![14]

He was cut down by cowardly murderers who hid in
the safety and protection of the woods with their guns.

Those migrant workers appeared to experience no
pain or suffering when the voice of their leader died, their
wilderness was so dense. Brutus acted behind a facade
of praise which in the end meant both the death of Caesar
and his own destruction. His facade so eroded he could
not stand to live with what he was—a defeated mur-
derer!

> Thanks be to God that Jesus did not turn away when His
> pain and suffering grew so great and intense!
> Thanks be to God that Christ did not forsake us when the
> rejection and persecution of His wilderness experience left
> Him so overwhelmed and lonely.
> Thanks be to God that Jesus Christ came to draw us unto
> Himself like sheep without a shepherd, like defenseless,
> flighty baby chicks!
> Thanks be to God that Jesus looked behind that facade of
> praise to see His Father's holy purpose!
> Thanks be to God that we can hear and heed the call to
> genuine praise
> authentic hosannas
> life-changing commitment and
> unending loyalty!
> Thanks be to God that even though entering Jerusalem
> meant death for Christ, He was willing to go in the wake
> of the facade of praise to complete His wilderness experi-
> ence!

Thanks be to God that we know we are to follow Christ, even though it means death to ourselves!

The journey is before us yet—so may we abandon the face of praise and embark on the next chapter of our own wilderness experience as we grow in faithfulness to Jesus!

Listening
Introspection
Seeking
Following
These concepts are foreign to the thinking of people.
Many contemporary religious people feel
    the patriarchs have come and gone
    the pioneer days have passed
    the theological struggles have been resolved
    the thorny issues have been settled.
The truth is each Christian needs inner searching and growth.
Religious faith cannot be gained by osmosis
                     heredity
                     tradition
                     exposure or
                     association.
God is calling new followers to journey with Him
             to risk a desert experience
          to travel the route of spiritual maturity.
Will you go?
Will you heed God's call to the wilderness?
If so—let's go!
If not—why?

7

Answering the Wilderness Call

A cartoon pictured a little boy and his friend standing at the front door of his home. The little tyke pointed to the doormat with the word WELCOME written on it. Proudly he announced to his younger friend, "That's the first thing I learned to read. It says 'Wipe your feet.'" The little boy had gotten the message his mother had translated to him—the only problem was, he did not have the mat's message! His misunderstanding is a parable of contemporary mankind. People are answering the calls given them by others without even knowing what the message means, what the sign says, or what they are called to do!

New records for business failures and bankruptcies are being set for this era of our nation's history. While there are numerous reasons for a financial difficulty in our day, it appears that a store-front sign may have captured much of our present malady. The sign simply read, "Gone out of business because we didn't know what our business was."

If we are honest with ourselves, we will admit that many times we have reached a point in our lives as workers, as students, as retired persons, and as family members when we felt totally frustrated because we did not know what we were doing or why we were doing it. We have to face the reality that our American society is a vast and complex network in which we can become enmeshed and lose ourselves. We fail to sense our place and find our niche of purpose and meaning. Indeed, we feel baffled by the business called life and find ourselves sinking into a deep cavity of fear, meaningless, and boredom. Many not only fail to know what the business of their lives is supposed to be but have also lost the desire to dream and plan.

The great Polish scientist and astronomer Copernicus lived over 500 years ago. Mankind had accepted for centuries the idea that the earth was the unmoving center of the universe. Copernicus disputed that theory and proved that the earth is a moving planet, not the center of the universe. For his views and teachings, this brilliant man was spurned by the church, and his writings were suppressed. He dreamed of the world's knowing the truth about the universe, yet all his life he was ignored and abused because of his dream. He lay on his deathbed when his first and only work was published. In spite of the public's reaction to his knowledge, Copernicus was faithful to his dream. On his tombstone are carved the words he chose:

> I do not seek a kindness equal to that given to Paul. Nor do I
> ask the grace granted to Peter. But that forgiveness which
> Thou didst grant to the robber—that, earnestly I crave.[1]

Copernicus was clearly an humble man of faith who maintained his dream in spite of the hatred and persecution received from the world virtually all his life. Now he is recognized as the founder of modern astronomy, but he lived his life in isolation and misunderstanding. He answered in faith the call to enter into an unexplored wilderness of knowledge which he mastered, but his peers rejected him because they refused to answer their own wilderness call to stretch their minds.

Over the centuries there have been the dreamers
                    those who reject the dream and
                the ones who are not aware of any dreams.
One person who did not know about dreams was talking to a book collector whom he told he had just thrown away an old Bible that had been in the family for generations. The man had concluded the Bible was of no value because it had been

packed away in his attic for years. He added that someone named "Guten-something" had printed the Bible.

The book collector gasped, "Not Gutenberg! My word, you have thrown away one of the first books ever printed! Did you not know that a copy recently sold for one million dollars at an auction?"

The non-dreamer would not be altered by that outburst. He countered, "My Bible would not have been worth anything. Some fellow named Martin Luther had owned it, and he had written all over it."[2]

We all have encountered people like this in our lifetime—
people who have all the answers
people who have no vision
people who refuse to dream
people who have never responded to their wilderness call.

Many of these people live their lives blindly with a grinding sense of compulsion and an utter absence of response to the call of God to be purposeful. Many people are running busily around in their workaholic routines, being eaten up by fear, anger, and greed, never fully understanding what is happening or how to escape. There are enormous feelings of futility and frustration in those who are caught in their web and are searching for a better way.

If answering the wilderness call means venturing forth in faith into a new frontier, why should we answer the wilderness call? Over seventeen centuries ago an Egyptian named Anthony heard a sermon on Matthew 19:21, "Go and sell what you own and give the money to the poor . . . then come and follow me."

In his own desire to be free of the meaningless web in which he was encased, he withdrew into a desert and lived in solitude for twenty years. When he emerged, people realized that he was whole in spirit, mind, and body. After he had been through the wilderness experience of having his outer shell cracked and had allowed the Spirit of Christ to dwell in him, people could see from his physical presence that he had been with Jesus! And thus people came from near and far to receive from him comfort, direction, healing, and hope. Anthony lived to the age of 106, and he is known as the founder of the Desert Fathers and Mothers, those Christians who gained the inner strength in the desert to witness against the evil of their world and to witness for the saving power of Jesus Christ. In the midst of overwhelming evil

> paralyzing compulsion
> seducing fear
> debilitating anger and
> astounding assault against their Lord

they sought to swim for their lives away from the sinking ship of their society. And in their response to their wilderness call, they were also able to salvage the moral, intellectual, and spiritual fabric of their society! Three important factors that shaped the lives of Anthony and those who followed in that way were: the discipline of solitude

> the discipline of silence and
> the discipline of unceasing prayer.

It is vital that we learn these disciplines in our day, though not necessarily in the same form the Desert Fathers practiced them. Our choice of teachers and mentors is more significant now than ever before because there are so many who grasp at the chance of teaching us in a self-centered, perverted manner.

There is a smothering desperation that has crowded into the lives of so many people! Many are so anxious to find a means of ceasing the pounding within them that they lunge at anyone and anything in hopes of finding help and release. Often in the process, the wrong course is chosen, and the solutions become worse than the original problems. The ancient story is told of a shoemaker who was unable to find work in his own town. Desperate because of his impoverished condition, he went to another town and opened not a shoe shop but a medical practice! By selling a drug he pretended was an antidote for all poison and disease, he achieved some success. Through much advertising of his solution, he grew both famous and wealthy.

Then one day the self-professed doctor became ill. The mayor of the town decided to test the honesty of this new doctor. He got a cup and pretended to mix poison with the man's healing medicine. Then he commanded the ill man to drink the deadly cup. The shoemaker feared he would die and confessed that he knew nothing of medicine! When he had finished telling his amazing story, the mayor called a meeting and told the townspeople they were more guilty than the impostor! They had entrusted their lives to a man no one would hire to make shoes for their feet! The shoemaker-turned-medicine-man had now lost his job, integrity, and self-esteem. His second problem was worse than his first!

When we determine to break loose from our besetting problems and answer God's call to embark on new experiences, we will seek to create newness of harsh places

> to live with the starkness of unfulfilled dreams
> to struggle through the remote and barren regions of
> our lives where the disappointments, pains, and
> wounds are hidden out of view.

A wilderness can be both good and bad. The key to

> creativity in life
> dreaming possible dreams
> distinguishing between the worthy and the fake

lies in the positive use of the wilderness motif as a means of growing spiritually and intellectually. There is a call from God to each human being to be on a journey toward wholeness and wellness. He wants people boldly and joyfully to embrace life and live it as He intended. But the world has been polluted with false ideas and phony "medicine men" who sell quick cures for serious problems. So, to hear God's clear word we must shut our ears to the noises of the world and quietly retreat

> to a place where God's voice can be deciphered and
> to a place where we can hear His clear direction.

We already are in a wilderness characterized by immorality

> injustice
> heartache

hatred
hostility
retribution
destruction
greed.

God calls us to stand still in the wilderness and watch and
listen for Him. He is there and wants to meet us

to teach us
to mold us
to shape us
to strengthen us.

To answer the wilderness call does not mean that we literally go and live in a desert. It does mean that we abandon all
the substitutes for God that we depend on to give our lives
substance, strength, and direction. It does mean we quit pre-
tending and begin living for God and in God! It does mean we
become willing to be disciplined by the Lord and molded into
vessels fit for meaningful service.

In the powerful concluding section of Hebrews there is a
model for our answering the wilderness call:

> So Jesus also suffered outside the gate in order to sanctify the
> people through his own blood. Therefore let us go forth to
> him outside the camp, bearing abuse for him.[3]

By Jewish law Jesus could not be put to death in the Holy
City, Jerusalem, so the authorities carried Him outside the
gate to Calvary for His murder. His going outside the protection of the city gate of Jerusalem was a reminder of people
who had dared to go beyond the gate of the portable city of
the Israelites during the wilderness wandering. Their only protection was to be found by remaining within the camp behind
the gates that had been erected. Some who dared to venture
outside the gates were never seen or heard of again. Therefore, the tendency of the Hebrew people was to stay "within
the gate."

Those ancient ones thought that God was to be found in
the holy place where the Ark of the Covenant was. To leave

the camp, in their estimation, was to leave security
>> to leave comfort they knew
>> to leave God Himself!

But do you perceive what God's preacher in Hebrews really said?

"Therefore"—that little big word in Greek that takes only three Greek letters to write—

"Therefore"—in light of the sacrifice Christ made on our behalf outside the camp beyond the gate,

"Therefore let us go forth to him outside the camp, bearing abuse for him."

God wants us to answer the wilderness call! And in answering we do not go into the darkness of the world blindly or alone. We "go forth to him" who has gone before us
>> in living
>> in suffering
>> in ministering
>> in obeying God!

When we answer the wilderness call we lay ourselves in the hands of God who goes before us
>> who goes behind us
>> who goes beside us
>> who goes within us

assuring us that what we now see and have is not lasting—we seek that city which is to come, the New Jerusalem, the Holy City, the place Christ declares He already has prepared for us! Thus, we can dare lay our lives on the line for Christ now because we know He holds the future!

As we contemplate answering the wilderness call, we can examine some of the numerous examples of noted biblical giants who left their normal, comfortable routine to go apart outside the camp and enter the wilderness.

Moses spent forty years in the wilderness before returning to Egypt.

John the Baptist spent most of his life in the wilderness.

Paul spent at least two years in the wilderness before initiating his missionary work.

Our Lord Himself was in the wilderness forty days and nights.

Abraham left his home in Ur at the age of seventy-five to go into a wilderness.

Genesis 12 tells us the story of his leaving home with Sarai, his wife. He was seventy-five and she was sixty-five. What a beautiful picture of a couple who heard God together, responded to God together, followed God together! One spouse never goes far in answering the wilderness call without the other spouse! Therefore, it is important that a couple draw near to God so they can draw near to each other so they can together heed God's call to obedience!

What makes Abram's and Sarai's answer to the wilderness call even more amazing is that God promised to make him the father of a nation—and at that time Abraham had no son! Eleven years later a son was born to Sarai's slave, Hagar. This event only heightened the frustration and disappointment of this couple who had heard a call and obediently responded to it. They left a wealthy, settled life and willingly became nomads in the wilderness in response to God. He had profound lessons for them to learn, and such education is time-consuming. When Abram was ninety-nine and Sarai was eighty-nine, God told them He would give them a son and through him Abram would become the father of a nation. Sarai laughed when she heard that news!

Possibly it was because they would be one hundred and ninety respectively or because they had given up on God's original promise!

God was not outdone. He changed their original names of Abram and Sarai to the more kingly names of Abraham and Sarah and instructed them the son would be named Isaac, meaning "he laugh."[4]

Finally Isaac was born! The wilderness experience began to assume a spiritual meaning, and the obedient couple began to sense the wonder of Yahweh and to comprehend their part in His plan. But then the underbrush of the wilderness closed in about them when God sent Abraham up a mountain and asked him to sacrifice his beloved son! Can you imagine the darkness that settled in the soul of Abraham?

He had waited so long for the divine promise to come true.

He had left the security of his cultured home for a wilderness.

He had sought to establish the worship of the One True God.

He had begun to walk out of one wilderness and was about to enter another one!

Can you imagine how Abraham felt as he started up the mountain that day? Every father who loves his son can surely sense the feelings that flooded God's faithful follower that awesome morning! They were going so high up the mountain they would be above the tree line, so Abraham had Isaac carry the wood that he would use to build the fire for his sacrifice. In that picture of the obedient son and the agonizing father we recognize God and His Son, Jesus Christ. Just as Abraham's son carried the wood up the mountain for his sacrifice, so centuries later God's Son would carry the wooden cross up Calvary's mountain for His sacrifice, a sacrifice that would make possible redemption of all people!

If Abraham had not already gone out of the protective camp into the wilderness with God, he could not have gone up the mountain to sacrifice his only son who could carry on the family line! But since Abraham had already obeyed and followed God's direction, we can appreciate the sincerity and the severity of what he did that day! God tested Abraham to see if he were willing to elevate Isaac as the god of his life, replacing the One, True God. And Abraham passed his test with flying colors! When God knew that Abraham had not made his son his god, another sacrifice was provided, and God and Abraham continued on their journey together, the journey that was born in the wilderness and would continue through the wilderness.

Can you imagine what it would be like to spend twenty-five years wandering in the wilderness with an unfulfilled promise as Abraham and Sarah did? Similarly, can you imag-

ine the concern Moses felt for his people the forty years he
was in the wilderness? However, there was something significant occurring in the lives of those wilderness wanderers that
prepared them for the most exciting dimension of their lives.
The key to Abraham and Sarah's response to the wilderness
call was that they learned to lay aside all their facades and see
God for who He is. For the Israelites leaving Egypt it required
longer to answer their wilderness call, but in each case God
could not use them until they were in communion with Him.
The time of God's seeming silence may have appeared to be
long, but the whole point was: God could not speak to them
or use them until they were silent enough to hear God!

We are now aware that one's brain has two separate parts
and functions. The left side controls the right hand and the
body's activity. The right side of the brain controls the left hand
and dreaming, meditating, and reflecting. Current research has
demonstrated that those people who are primarily using the
left side of their brain are almost hyperactive, while those who
rely mainly on the right side are relaxed and calm. Abraham
and Moses appear to be ancient examples of activists who
needed time in the wilderness in order to get in touch with the
unused portion of their brain. Only when they became whole
in their solitude were they able to dream God's dream and
become religious visionaries.

So many of us settle for less than what God is trying to
give us when He challenges us to answer our wilderness call.
With this outlook we come to the church's buildings and even
take membership with the feeling that is all we are to do or are
expected to do. Without any helps for making the journey
through the wilderness, people seem to remain satisfied
to stand on the fringe of the Christian life
    to see the parade of religious excitement
        to hear those who have touched the Lord
            to have their emotions stirred and then
                to go home the same person who came!
Our activism often prevents our full surrender to and dependence on God's call to us in Jesus Christ. We are so anxious

to do, to impress, to please . . . that we fail to trust Christ to do what He is exceedingly able to do and what He desires to do and for us *to be* what is pleasing to Christ!

Solitude denotes some privacy or quietness. But for the Desert Fathers of the Scripture and early Church, solitude was the place of death to the old self and the emergence of a new person through life-changing conversion. Solitude was the experience of becoming honest and open before God and thus discovering Who He was. There is a struggle within us because all the efforts to maintain our false selves exert themselves any and every time we seek to become complete before God. The struggle is real, and the wisdom of the wilderness is that we cannot emerge victorious in our own strength. We overcome our feelings of nothingness when we give ourselves wholly and completely to the Lord Jesus Christ! In our self-giving to Christ we can envision how Christ sees us and can dream His dreams for us.

Sometimes dreams of who we are to be and what we are to do die because they were the wrong dreams. Other times dreams die because we lacked the commitment to our dreams. But there are times our dreams die because we lack the compatriots to see those dreams become reality. How sad it is that often "good men do nothing" while the evil men derail any and every dream that would bring people
closer to Christ
  close to one another
    closer to their potential
      closer to the glory of God!

A dreamer is one who has heard the wilderness call and is willing to follow Christ wherever He leads. It may come as a surprise to you that the prophet Joel proclaimed in 2:28 that when God's Spirit has been poured out on His people "old men shall dream dreams" and "young men shall see visions." Remember that the apostle John did not do his best dreaming when he was a young man with the Master. John did his best dreaming when he was an old man exiled on the island of Patmos! Why? Because in the wilderness experience of exile on Patmos, John practiced openness to his God and readiness to be His instrument of proclamation. He dared to open himself fully to Christ after the heavy force of the world's evil had been thrown against him. Holy dreams come from God into lives that are possessed by God's Spirit.

Dreamers dare take risks! The basic premise in the theology of risk is that God is looking for people who do not know it cannot be done! God's Spirit is asking us to do things we refuse to do on our own, though the Holy Spirit would work His miracle in us if only we would risk carrying out God's dream for us. God wants people to be willing to dream and to risk doing the unthinkable when He commands it, even if that means climbing out on a limb someone else is shaking with no one down below to catch us!

God gave Abraham a test on the mountain with Isaac to see if he trusted God's power and provision. Centuries later Christ gave His disciples a test recorded in John 6 to see if they trusted His power and provision. After the disciples had been with Jesus for a brief time on an isolated hillside, a multitude surrounded Him.

In John 6:5 Jesus asked Philip, "How are we to buy bread, so that these people may eat?" John carefully notes in verse 6 that this was Philip's test to see if he trusted Jesus' ability to provide, and Philip failed! He did not answer Jesus' question. Philip figured that the daily wages of 200 working men would not be adequate. Jesus was asking where they would go to get food for a total gathering of men, women, and children numbering in excess of ten thousand people. Philip responded with how much it would take and thus how impossible it would be. How saddened this must have made Jesus! He wanted to see if Philip could admit, while it was impossible for him, with Him all things are possible! So convinced of what could *not* be done, Philip ignored what Christ could do! He had no dream of Christ's miracle that day, so he refused to answer the wilderness call and remained safely within the camp that gave him his accustomed security.

We see a second test in verses 8-9. Andrew brought to

Jesus a boy who had a small, one-person lunch. He had five loaves of bread and two fish. Those five "loaves" were probably flat, hard, pancake-like bread, and the fish were perhaps little, pickled, sardine-like fish. Andrew's question reflects his lack of risk-taking: "But what are they among so many?" So miserably did Andrew fail that Jesus never answered him! He told the disciples to seat the multitudes and after He had blessed them, He distributed an overabundance of food through His great miracle! When all had eaten "as much as they wanted" the disciples gathered up the leftovers which amounted to twelve baskets full of food! Our Lord did not need much of an opening for His miracle—just one trusting little boy who answered his call of the Lord in the wilderness! But His disciples would not venture from their comfortable viewpoints. Andrew was figuring in minimums while

Jesus was figuring in maximums!

Philip was calculating the possible while

Jesus was calculating the impossible!

Our Lord is a specialist in the impossible, but He does not force Himself upon us. It takes an act of faith on our part to leave the camp and answer the wilderness call so the windows of heaven can be opened for our miracle to be given us! And it requires our attentive listening to sense where God is and where His Spirit is leading us.

Helps for listening to God's call and the means for answering the wilderness call are found in solitude, meditation, and silence.

The psalmist declared in 62:1, "For God my soul waits in silence. . . ." Solitude, meditation, and silence are all components of the prayer we risk praying when we dream holy dreams and follow our Lord into the wilderness where He has already gone before us. Meditation enables us to focus on God and silence is the completion of solitude. Words often become both empty and bothersome. We are constantly bombarded by words. All day long we see words and hear words. At last it seems that such a flood of words has washed away any meaning for words spoken or heard. Most of us know the experience of having long talks with someone and then feeling when it was over the unsettling desire that most of those words had been left unspoken. We know the inner pain of telling others about ideas and feelings, thinking they wanted to know, only in the end to discover that no one cared or understood. Words can cause us to mire down in the expectation and response of others. When we cease being so dependent on words to fill the place of our empty personhood, we can enjoy silence, as well as silence with others.

It can be unnerving not to rely on words to defend ourselves and to fill the silence. But the fact is that silence guards and nurtures the inner spiritual fire of the Holy Spirit. One Christian of ancient times observed:

> When the door of the steambath is continually left open, the heat inside rapidly escapes through it; likewise the soul, in its desire to say many things, dissipates its remembrance of God through the door of speech, even though everything it says may be good.[5]

In a world in which the "in" word in "sharing," it becomes all the more difficult, but necessary, for us to tend our spiritual fire often enough that we do not dampen our interior fire. In a time when there are more lost wanderers than ever, we need to have a warm and bright fire within for those who search for God.

Vincent van Gogh, the nineteenth-century Dutch painter, knew the temptation to keep the door of his outer life constantly open through busy activity for all who passed by to see the fire and not merely smoke in the chimney. But he realized that if he did that, the fire would only die and no one would be able to experience warmth from his inner spiritual fire. His life stands as an impressive witness of his faithfully maintaining his inner life though, in the process, he did miss "sharing" with others. Now we know that in the course of his lifetime no one came to warm by his spiritual or artistic fire, but in the last half-century many thousands have been comforted and inspired by his paintings, drawings, and writings.[6]

We are still tempted to avoid solitude and silence, when in fact they teach us to speak, to feel, and to live with our hearts.

In the classical biblical sense, *heart* refers to the whole person. When we feel and live with our heart, we are communicating our entire being. But we are not able to so live without answering the wilderness call to solitude and silence.

Solitude and silence lead us to pray—"to pray without ceasing."[7]

Instead of viewing prayer as a divine ouija board which we can manipulate

Instead of considering prayer as a mental exercise in which we can understand and then control God

prayer of the heart is the experience in which we hide nothing from God and submit ourselves totally to His merciful love. Prayer of the heart is the only means by which we can approach the merciful God as an admitted sinner. There is great power in such prayer—

not power to manipulate and change God

but power to transform and change us!

As the force of the undertow of the ocean can sweep the most powerful swimmer away in a moment, so through a prayer of repentance and desire to know God we can be swept into the flow with Him and see His will for His world.

Matthew and Luke record that Jesus took a wilderness journey following His baptism. It was a very high moment for Jesus following His public identification of His ministry and the divine affirmation He received from His Heavenly Father: "Thou art my beloved Son; with thee I am well pleased."[8]

The next three years would prove to be difficult from every possible standpoint. It was significant that the Holy Spirit led Christ into the wilderness for forty days, so He might fast and have uninterrupted time to strengthen the experience of solitude, silence, and unceasing prayer. Here He set the pattern that gained the commitment which provided the strength He needed across the most difficult days of His life.

If there ever were a busy person, Christ was that person! But in His wilderness experience He learned the discipline of

taking time to pray, taking time to be alone, taking time to
tend His inner fire, taking time to give His Father praise,
honor, and glory. The discipline of prayer has never been
easy. The Desert Fathers learned what Jesus meant when He
talked about losing life while trying to save it. Only when we
give up ownership of life and accept it as it comes are we able
to offer thanks to God and live fully all our days. Through
their discipline of unceasing prayer, those early Christians were
able to live in the Spirit and let life flow without trying to control or manipulate it. They depended on God to guide and
strengthen them in every situation. They discovered that life,
like an arrow that would be shot, must be drawn back before it
can be shot forward. If the arrow is not pulled back, it merely
falls limp to the ground. We will never live life to our fullest
potential unless we are continually withdrawing to our Source
of power. Too few Christians practice the kind of withdrawal in
prayer that makes needed strength available. We need to stop
our aimless chatter and be drawn back into the power of God
that would propel us into the world in His strength and name.

Across the centuries, Christians have practiced repeating
one-sentence prayers, most often drawn from the Scripture.
Sometimes in the very repetition of a powerful prayer, one can
be drawn away from the thoughts and snares of the world into
the heart so God can be fully met. Some helpful examples of
such prayers are:

> "I love thee, O Lord."—Psalm 18:1
> "Lord Jesus Christ, have mercy on me."—Matthew 15:22
> "The Lord is my shepherd."—Psalm 23:1
> "Do not forsake me, O Lord!"—Psalm 38:21
> "Father, all things are possible with Thee."—Mark 14:36
> "O God, be not far from me."—Psalm 71:12
> "Into thy hand I commit my spirit."—Psalm 31:5
> "Not my will but thine be done."—Matthew 26:39
> "Create in me a clean heart, O God."—Psalm 51:10
> "Be gracious to me, O God."—Psalm 109:1
> "Thy kingdom come."—Matthew 6:10
> "Thy will be done."—Matthew 6:10
> "My God will supply every need."—Philippians 4:19

"Help, Lord!"—Psalm 12:1
"Save me, O God!"—Psalm 69:1
"Redeem me."—Psalm 69:18
"Teach me thy way, O Lord."—Psalm 86:11
"Search me, O God."—Psalm 139:23
"Guard me, O Lord."—Psalm 140:4
"Come, Lord Jesus."—Revelation 22:20
"Deliver me, O Lord."—Psalm 120:2
"Praise the Lord!"—Psalm 113:1
"Jesus."—Luke 4:1

If and when we are willing to pray repeatedly such a prayer
ten to twenty minutes a day before making our requests
known to God, it is possible we will begin

to break through our facades

to pray from the heart and

to answer God's call into and through the wilderness!
Then, "Happy are the pure in heart for they shall see God,"[9]
may truly become real to us! Praying as we answer the wilderness call will enable us to live in calmness with a pure heart in
the midst of a restless world. We must take care not to mis-
read the signs that are before us. Rather, we need to exercise
the courage to break out of our protective shells and embark
on our wilderness journey.

Three men used to visit old Anthony once a year. Two
talked much about their salvation and thoughts. The third
never said anything. After several years Anthony commented
one day that the third never asked anything. This quiet man
replied, "It is enough to see you."[10] Solitude, meditation, and
silence are adequate when we sense God's nearness as we are
in the presence of a person journeying faithfully through their
wilderness call! Could it be if we answered the wilderness call
that people could look at us and tell we have been with Jesus
and therefore feel a strength and blessing just to be in
our presence? It is possible.

This is the business of those who follow Christ.

Join in this pilgrimage of answering the wilderness call!

The Wilderness Experience . . .

Lonely	Reflective
Devastating	Renewing
Frightening	Calming
Painful	Restful
Grieving	Growing
Disabling	Strengthening
Stressful	Relaxing

Each person has many wilderness experiences—
   some are positive and others are negative.
The outcome of our wilderness experience depends on
   our attitude toward life
      our choice of response
         our relationship with Christ
            our openness to growth
               our desire for obedience
                  our sensitivity to support systems
                     our responsiveness to the Spirit.

Many people have gone into the wilderness and died there!
Others have gone into the wilderness and come alive there!
Enter boldly, thoughtfully, openly, carefully, and may you
emerge stronger than when you entered! Brave Journey!

Afterword

I have written about the wilderness not from a technical or scholarly viewpoint but from a truly personal perspective! During the past several years I have had wilderness experiences I never imagined—
some chosen for growth through solitude
meditation and
silence
some entangled me through the ugly face of evil!
And in the dread of the wilderness the
darkness has been oppressive
stress has been overwhelming
shock about people's inhumanity to others has been staggering
destructiveness of evil has been astounding
pain of grief has been cutting
force of character attack has been oppressive
cloud of anxiety has been smothering
pressure of threats has been debilitating.

I have stood with pilgrims when their loved one was suffering with painful, terminal illness. I have watched while older friends had to give up job, house, car, and freedom. While I remember the weariness of my younger student years, I never imagined possible the exhausting, paralyzing impact of repeated wildernesses in my life!

No longer do I just watch people struggle in the

wilderness—for I, too, have been there! I have seen and felt
the starkness and loneliness
    the intensity and despair
        the destruction and devastation.
I have also felt God's uplifting presence in
                    the silence and the awesomeness
                        the beauty and the joy
                            the calm and the peace.
    Some cultures use a physical wilderness experience for
males as a rite of passage from childhood to adulthood. When
a boy entered the wilderness and survived, he came out a
man! Without a doubt after we have endured the wilderness,
we gain a maturity that readies us for a life of growth and service not otherwise possible! We do not always seek the wilderness, for often the wilderness erupts in the path before us. The
only way for us to attain our intended purpose is to journey
through the wilderness. Through my wilderness experiences I
have learned things about myself and about my Lord there I
never imagined possible! The Father's message of hope and
encouragement may come to us in unexpected ways and
places, but always at exactly the right time. On a particularly
dark and lonely day I found His message to me on a wall
hanging in a neighboring church:

                    Though the storm
                        May hide the rainbow
                    And the night
                        May hide the dawn
                    Because we know
                        God loves us
                    Our hearts
                        Go singing on!

    As I assure you of where I have been
                    where I am and
                    where I shall be
I remind you that you can discover your best times of growth
in the midst of your wilderness experience! With God's

strength you can endure the worst of the negative wilderness. With your effort you can learn the discipline of chosen aloneness that will afford your best opportunity to know and obey God. That wilderness need not be an isolated desert. It may be a quiet place in your home, an unused chapel in your church building, a wooded place in the neighborhood or park.

Jesus understood the importance of an extended quiet time, an intense preparatory time, in order to know the strength of and communion with His Father. You need to employ the same approach in your spiritual walk, that you might discover the fullness of God's love for you and His power within you.

Robert Browning penned words long ago that well describe the perspective I have gained in the wilderness.

> If I stoop
> Into a dark tremendous sea of cloud
> It is but for a time. I press God's lamp
> Close to my breast; its splendor soon or late
> Will pierce the gloom; I shall emerge one day.[1]

The wilderness is before you—it has many shapes and form. Lay fear aside—

Take the Father's hand—

And journey bravely!

You, too, will emerge—one day!

Notes

Introduction
   1. R. Earl Allen, *Strength from Shadows* (Nashville: Broadman Press, 1967), p. 17.
   2. Ibid.
   3. *The American Heritage Dictionary of the English Language* (New York: Houghton Mifflin Company, 1969), p. 1465.
   4. Deuteronomy 1:19.
   5. Deuteronomy 1:21.
   6. Job 12:24.
   7. Jeremiah 9:2.
   8. Isaiah 35:1.
   9. Isaiah 51:3.
  10. Isaiah 40:3.

Chapter 1   "Crisis in the Wilderness"
   1. Dale Evans Rogers, *God in the Hard Times* (Waco: Word Books, Publisher, 1984), pp. 22-24.
   2. Frank Stagg, "Matthew," *The Broadman Bible Commentary* (Nashville: Broadman Press, 1970), Vol. 8, pp. 98-99.
   3. Matthew 4:3.
   4. Matthew 4:6.
   5. Malachi 3:1-2.
   6. Matthew 4:8-9.
   7. Matthew 28:18.
   8. Stagg, p. 98.
   9. Calvin Miller, *The Table of Inwardness* (Downers Grove, Ill.: Inter-varsity Press, 1984), p. 34.
  10. William and Carolyn S. Self, *Confessions of a Nomad* (Atlanta: Peachtree Publishers, Ltd., 1983). p. 110.
  11. Rogers, p. 98.
  12. Ibid., p. 7.
  13. Self, p. vii.

14. *Modern Men in Search of a Soul* (New York: Harcourt, Brace, 1933), p. 125; cited by Douglass V. Steere, *On Beginning Within* (New York: Harper & Row, Publishers, 1964), p. 9.

15. Bernard Baruch in Rogers, p. 11.

16. Robert Raines, *To Kiss the Joy* (Waco: Word Books, Publisher, 1973), pp. 23-24.

17. Soren Kierkegaard, *Purity of Heart Is to Will One Thing,* translated with an Introductory Essay by Douglass V. Steere (New York: Harper & Row, Publishers, 1948), p. 23.

18. Dietrich Bonhoeffer, *The Cost of Discipleship* (New York: The Macmillan Company, 1963), pp. 19-20.

19. Cited from *Thoughts in Solitude* by Thomas Merton (The Abbey of Our Lady of Gethsemane, 1958) in *You,* Mark Link (Allen, Tex: Argus Communications, 1976), p. 71.

20. Matthew 4:11.

21. Rogers, p. 37.

22. Self, p. 125.

23. Theresa of Avila in Steere, *On Beginning Within,* pp. 29-30.

Chapter 2   "The Trap of Wrong Answers"

1. Lloyd C. Douglas, *The Robe* (New York: Pocket Books, Inc., 1942), pp. 412-13.

2. Thomas Merton, *The Wisdom of the Desert* (New York: New Directions, 1960), p. 28.

3. Ibid., p. 43.

4. Genesis 2:19-23.

5. Genesis 2:23.

6. Genesis 3:1.

7. Genesis 3:6.

8. Genesis 3:12.

9. G. Henton Davies, *The Broadman Bible Commentary* (Nashville: Broadman Press, 1969), Vol. 1, pp. 139 ff.

10. Samuel Miller, *Man the Believer* (New York: Abingdon Press, 1968), pp. 44-45.

11. Merton, *The Wisdom of the Desert,* p. 31.

12. Dag Hammarskjold, *Markings* (New York: Alfred A. Knopf, 1964), p. 213.

13. Philippians 4:7.

14. John Killinger, *Bread for the Wilderness, Wine for the Journey* (Waco: Word Books, Publisher, 1976), p. 77.

15. Luke 4:1-2.

16. Deuteronomy 8:3.

17. Malcolm O. Tolbert, "Luke," *The Broadman Bible Commentary* (Nashville: Broadman Press, 1970), Vol. 9, p. 42.

18. G. Curtis Jones, *Strongly Tempted* (New York: The World Publishing Company, 1968), p. 122.

19. Matthew 28:20; Paul Lee Tan, *Encyclopedia of 7,700 Illustrations* (Rockville, Md.: Assurance Publishers, 1979), #3480, p. 814.

Chapter 3   "Bargaining with God"

1. Aesop, *The Fables of Aesop* (New York: A. L. Brent, Publisher, n.d.), pp. 266-67.

2. Harold S. Kushner, *When Bad Things Happen to Good People* (New York: Avon Books, 1981), p. 117.

3. Ibid., p. 111.

4. Robert W. Bailey, *Ministering to the Grieving* (Grand Rapids: Zondervan Press, 1981), p. 37.

5. 2 Chronicles 7:14.

6. John 3:16.

7. Harry Emerson Fosdick, *Dear Mr. Brown* (New York: Harper & Brothers, Publishers, 1961), p. 183.

8. Matthew 4:6.

9. Jesus quoted from Deuteronomy 6:16.

10. Isaiah 26:3-4.

11. Merton, *The Wisdom of the Desert*, p. 72.

12. Leslie Weatherhead, *That Immortal Sea* (New York: Abingdon Press, 1963), p. 44.

13. Kushner, p. 148.

14. Merton, *The Wisdom of the Desert*, p. 66.

15. Archibald MacLeish, *J.B.* (Boston: Houghton Mifflin Company, 1958), p. 153.

Chapter 4   "On Distinguishing the Voices"

1. Stephen Vincent Benet, *The Devil and Daniel Webster* (New York: Holt, Rinehart and Winston, 1965), p. 16.

2. Ibid., p. 48.

3. John Henry Jowett, *Springs* (Grand Rapids: Baker Book House, 1976), p. 49.

4. George Bernard Shaw, *Complete Plays with Prefaces*, Vol. 2, *Back to Methuselah* (New York: Dodd, Mead and Company, 1963), pp. 12-13.

5. Frank Stagg, "Matthew," *The Broadman Bible Commentary*, Vol. 8, p. 98; Malcolm O. Tolbert, "Luke," *The Broadman Bible Commentary*, Vol. 9, p. 43.

6. Leonard Griffith, *God's Time and Ours* (New York: Abingdon Press, 1964), p. 76.

7. Carlyle Marney, *Beggars in Velvet* (New York: Abingdon Press, 1960), p. 113.

8. *Proclaim*, January, 1984, Vol. 14, p. 35.

9. *Proclaim*, January, 1983, Vol. 13, p. 32.

10. William L. Stidger, *These Are Sermons in Stories* (New York: Abingdon Press, 1942), p. 66.

11. Ibid., pp. 66-67.

12. Merle Allison Johnson, *Christian Seasons* (Nashville: Abingdon Press, 1976), p. 105.

Chapter 5   "Spiritual Support System"

1. Edgar D. Jones, *Sermons I Love to Preach* (New York: Harper & Brothers, Publishers, 1953), p. 187.

2. Daniel 3:25.

3. Daniel 3:28.

4. Matthew 4:11.

5. *The Interpreter's Dictionary of the Bible,* Vol. 1, p. 129.

6. Acts 12:11.

7. Hebrews 13:2.

8. Billy Graham, *Angels: God's Secret Agents* (Garden City: Doubleday & Company, Inc., 1975), p. 87.

9. Ibid., pp. 89-90.

10. Psalm 91:11.

11. 2 Corinthians 2:11.

12. Ephesians 4:27.

13. 1 Peter 5:8.

14. James 4:7.

15. 2 Kings 6:16.

16. Graham, p. 168.

Chapter 6　　"Behind the Facade of Praise"

1. Act III, scene i, line 80.

2. Act III, scene ii, lines 70-71.

3. Act III, scene ii, lines 178-184.

4. Mark 6:4-6.

5. Mark 10:37.

6. Luke 22:24.

7. Psalm 55:14.

8. Psalm 55:21.

9. Holman Hunt in James Stewart, *Life & Teachings of Jesus* ((New York: Abingdon Press, n.d.), p. 135.

10. Leslie D. Weatherhead, *The Meaning of the Cross* (New York: Abingdon Press, 1948), p. 46.

11. Boris Pasternak, "Evil Days," *Modern Religious Poems* (New York: Harper & Row, Publishers, 1964), Jacob Trapp, editor, p. 120.

12. Mark 6:34.

13. Matthew 23:37-39.

14. John Steinbeck, *In Dubious Battle* (New York: Penguin Books, 1978), pp. 310 ff.

Chapter 7　　"Answering the Wilderness Call"

1. *Encyclopedia of 7700 Illustrations,* #2309, p. 571.

2. *The Rotarian,* December, 1985, p. 64.

3. Hebrews 13:12-13.

4. Genesis 17:17-21.

5. Henri J. M. Nouwen, *The Way of the Heart* (New York: The Seabury Press, 1981), pp. 52-53.

6. Ibid., p. 55.

7. 1 Thessalonians 5:17.

8. Luke 3:22.

9. Matthew 5:8.

10. Benedicta Ward, trans. *The Sayings of the Desert Fathers* (London: Mowbrays, 1975), p. 6.

Afterword
1. Walter B. Knight, *Knight's Master Book of New Illustrations* (Grand Rapids: Wm. B. Eerdmans Publishing Company, 1956), p. 474.